loving
yourself
more

virginia ann froehle, r.s.m.

loving
yourself
more

101 meditations for women

Illustrations by Doris Klein, C.S.A.

AVE MARIA PRESS
Notre Dame, Indiana 4655

First printing, August, 1993
Third printing, September, 1995
30,000 copies in print

© 1993 Ave Maria Press, Inc., Notre Dame, IN 46556

All rights reserved. No part of this book may be used or reproduced in any manner whatsoever without written permission, except in the case of reprints in the context of reviews.

International Standard Book Number: 0-87793-513-0

Library of Congress Catalog Card Number: 93-71890

Cover and text design by Elizabeth French

Printed and bound in the United States of America.

Dedication

To those members of my religious community (Sisters of Mercy) and my parish community (St. Aloysius Gonzaga), my family and friends who help me to receive the love of my God and to grow in loving myself

Contents

Introduction ———————————— 9

I Am Chosen by God ———————— 21

God Promises Good to Me ————— 43

God's Love and Faithfulness
   Enfold Me ———————————— 65

God's Mercy Cleanses Me ————— 87

God Strengthens Me ——————— 107

Introduction

"I'm just beginning to realize how little I love myself," Diane told the group as she stared at the floor. "I think I get healthy caring for myself mixed up with selfishness sometimes. I'm often not sure which is which."

"I've been doing everything I'm supposed to do for years," sighed Mary Beth. "Only recently I realized that what I am 'supposed to do' is take care of everyone else."

In the Thursday morning women's prayer group we talked about loving our neighbors as ourselves. Some of us discovered the words "as ourselves" as if we had just seen them for the first time. Do we love ourselves? How? Why don't we love ourselves? Can we love anyone else genuinely if we don't love ourselves? Who supports us in loving ourselves?

Marian continued the discussion by voicing her suspicion that she was too young when her parents tried to teach her some of their Christian ideals. "They urged me to love all other people, even if they were cranky, unfair, or indifferent toward me. They encouraged me to do what Jesus challenged everyone to do—love my neighbors, love even my enemies. I was so young, however, that pleasing my mom and dad was most important to me. So, without knowing what I was doing, I put down my need to take care of myself in order to act as though

I loved others. This meant I would do what others wanted and take care of them."

"I'm glad that my parents didn't lay the love-my-enemies thing on me so early," Terry responded, "but, as I grew up, it does seem that everyone always expected me, as a girl, to look out for family needs. They surely prepared me by expectation to care for aging parents, my husband and children, the sick, the grieving, the poor, the dog, the parakeet and then the local committee for recycling. A few years ago, I began feeling bent over, as if I were held down by weights. I've done a lot of changing to straighten up again."

Susan nodded. "My experience is similar. I was an adaptive child and I especially loved religion class. But after years of 'practicing' what I was taught, I recognized that I couldn't love my neighbor very well even though I truly wanted to. By this time, however, I had become a conscientious volunteer and care-giver, though my service often sprang from 'shoulds' and 'oughts' rather than from any loving freedom in my heart. Sometimes this was OK. No one always feels like doing what is needed. But I gave such service most of the time and I found myself in depression, a kind of burnout. Sometimes I felt bitter and just wanted to thumb a ride on the interstate, to get away, anywhere. Then I felt guilty about feeling these things."

"Doesn't our religion reinforce all this self-giving?" asked Diane. "We are told to lose ourselves so we can save ourselves. But obviously most of us don't feel saved in the way that is promised."

"And don't forget, 'Lay down your lives for one another,' and 'Take up your cross and follow me,'" added Jennifer who had been quiet so far.

The members agreed that women who were encouraged to love themselves as they were growing up were indeed blessed. Most of this group, however, felt that they had received little teaching or modeling of healthy self-care.

Some said that words like "loving yourself" or "taking care of yourself first" got stuck in their throats. The words translated as "selfish" or "self-centered" as they got scrambled around with the inner voices from the past. Some people in the present even reinforced the earlier tapes with a sarcastic, "Taking care of number one, eh?"

"We have a lot to learn about the difference between an unhealthy 'me-first' attitude and a healthy Christian love of self and others," concluded Susan.

Believing in God's Unconditional Love

Our discussions further revealed that many parents and early teachers had also taught about God's unconditional love, forgiveness, mercy, personal providence, and faithfulness. We agreed that we were glad for these teachings, that we believed in them, and that they helped to balance our lives.

"But do we believe?" someone asked.

"If I believe in God's unconditional love, why do I find myself trying to please God or catch myself bargaining for something I want?"

"If I believe in God's total forgiveness, why am I sometimes bothered by guilt? And why am I unable to forgive myself at times?"

"If I believe in God's mercy, why do I fear being judged even on my faults?"

"If I believe in God's personal providence and faithfulness, why do I worry?"

"If I believe that God loves me so much, why am I so down on myself sometimes? Why do I feel so unworthy? Why does my self-esteem get so low?"

What Is Asked of Us?

Jane pulled us even further into the gospel commands and our confusion about them. She reminded us that faith in Jesus' love demands even more from us. The command to "love your neighbor as yourself" which Jesus quoted from the Jewish scriptures gave way to Jesus' new law: "Love one another *as I have loved you*" (John 15:12). He said this after he finished washing the feet of his friends. Then he walked into torture, crucifixion, and death as an example of what he meant by love.

Jane made it clear that we are called to love and serve, even heroically. It was also clear that something was missing in the love and service we were giving: a love of self modeled by God's love for us. It was clear that, at present, love of self and love of others seemed to be in conflict. Everyone grew silent.

Then new thoughts emerged: Loving others as we love ourselves and loving others as we are loved by God intertwine. We can only begin to love ourselves by receiving the love we have been offered by God in Jesus—and in the persons who reflect that love to us. We began to see that we could only give as much love to our neighbors as we could give to ourselves.

How We Fail to Love Ourselves

In my pastoral work outside the prayer group, I meet many women who struggle with lack of self-love in other ways. Since they do not value themselves, they do not think others will value them, so they isolate themselves, refusing to make many friends or become part of a group. They fear offering an opinion or a service, thinking it will be rejected.

Other women go bravely forward for a while. Then they find themselves caught in an addiction to alcohol, prescription drugs, overeating, compulsive spending, compulsive talking, or sexual promiscuity. They may feel trapped in abusive relationships. Perhaps because of their own abusive backgrounds, they struggle to keep from hurting their own children.

Some women try to give themselves value in their own eyes or the eyes of others by bragging, by pushing position and career success above everything else, by showing off stylish clothes and other possessions. Some go beyond assertiveness and attack others verbally. They may treat others shabbily at work, as if to say, "I'll reject you before you reject me."

Can all this be blamed on lack of self-love? No, our lives and personalities are not that simple. Severe problems and intense suffering underlie all these symptoms. But part of each problem is a lack of self-respect, a lack of healthy care for self. All these problems reveal a lack of self-love. All recovery calls for growth in love of self.

Meditating on God's Love

So how do we come to love ourselves more? The prayer group members agreed that meditating on God's complete, unconditional love for us as individuals, as well as a community, would be a start.

Enter this book. I hope that it will help all of us who need to grow in loving ourselves as God loves us. It invites us first to meditate on scripture passages proclaiming God's love for us. Then during some prayer time, we can let God's messages soak in, let the words seep through our pores, let the Spirit of God rise up in our spirits.

These meditations do not attempt to cover all the Christian mysteries. They invite us to focus only on the first, God's love for us and God's call to us to love ourselves.

If we grow in loving ourselves as God in Jesus loves us, we can freely offer love and service to others. We will be free to sacrifice ourselves in following Jesus to the cross when this call comes.

We will be able to participate happily in contributing to the reign of God for which Jesus prayed. We will also be able to receive the fruit of Jesus' promise, ". . . that they may have life and have it abundantly" (John 10:10).

Meditating with This Book

Prepare: Set aside five or ten minutes to relax your mind and body before meditating. This can be prayer in itself. You will come prepared to let the word of God enter into you.

Read the Bible passage: Each meditation begins with a Bible passage. Its citation accompanies it, so that you can find and read the whole passage, chapter, or book if you wish.

Reflect: Your reflection on the passage is most important. I have offered a few thoughts to help you begin your own reflection. The more you can connect the words and events of the Bible to the particular events, desires, crises, feelings, and decisions of your life, the more the scriptures will come alive in you.

Pray: At the end of each meditation is a one-line prayer or affirmation entitled "For Your Day." Repeating it throughout the day will sustain your meditation. Often the line seems to need a name of God at the end. Since people use many names and images, I usually have left out any form of address, even the word God. I suggest adding your name or image for God at the beginning or end.

Reading and Praying with Scripture

When we read the Bible, we can do so in several ways. We can read for the *historical* meaning of the passage. When we do this we try to find out what the literal meaning of the passage was when it was written. Scholars today have a wide variety of scientific tools to discover this meaning and their findings are available to us in various types of resources.

Another way to read the Bible is to learn the *community's story.* Most—though not all—of the Bible passages spoken in God's name are addressed to communities. To understand their meaning, we need to know the story behind them.

Yet, individuals make up the community, so each individual must also hear the words personally if a community is going to respond. Thus the third way we can read the books of the Bible is in the context of our *personal stories.* Each of us brings a personal life experience to our understanding of the passages, personalities, and stories. Finding our personal connections brings the Bible to life in our daily lives. This book offers passages for meditation and prayer to help you discover your own story, not to enable Bible study. I have selected the quotations and written the reflections to be read or heard by individuals who bring their own personal stories to them. The Bible passages are paraphrased to reflect the personal meaning or call of the passage. My hope is that all of us as individuals will bring the fruit of our meditations to the community(ies) to which we belong.

Remember that the Bible comes out of a patriarchal society, that is, one whose religion, economics, and politics are controlled by men. The books of the Bible are generally written by men for men and about men's concerns. Women were to receive the word of God through their fathers and their husbands. Because of this, many women and some men today face difficult decisions. Some have rejected the Bible altogether because of others who use it to claim that patriarchy is God's will, a structure for all times. Others believe that the patriarchy is cultural and not of divine inspiration. The latter hold that the truths revealed by the Spirit of God are beyond any social structures and they are given to women and men alike.

Yet those who choose to accept the messages of the Bible recognize that a passage addressed to "men" and "brothers" isn't conveying its meaning to the whole human race. For this reason, the paraphrased passages use only inclusive language.

Consider Your Image of God

God is spirit. God is neither male nor female, mother nor father, sister nor brother, vine nor rock, bakerwoman nor shepherd. These words are all images or metaphors by which we try to picture God or relate to some quality of God. God is, of course, more than any of our images. In fact, to hold on to any one image—visual or relational—as the only image is to make an idol. This is against the first commandment. It puts something false between us and God.

We need to choose our images of God carefully. Some of our difficulties in believing in God's constant and unconditional love come from having inadequate images of God. In the New Testament the most frequently used image of God is father. Depending on the relationship we had with early significant male figure(s) in our lives, the image of God as Father will provoke a variety of responses in us. Our ability to trust in God's love is directly related to the trust we were able to have in that special person's love for us. But since no father or father-figure is perfect, we may need to examine and sometimes change or modify our image.

With greater frequency women and men choose feminine as well as masculine images of God for prayer. So God becomes mother, wisdom, friend, source of courage, sister, the one who searches us out, the one who offers unconditional forgiveness and so on.

Using masculine images of God leads us to expect from God the kind of relationship we have with men. Experiencing the feminine leads us to expect from God the kind of relationship we have with women. In each image, we touch and relate to a different aspect of God.

Most of us have many images of God. We pray to God in the psalms, in prayers and hymns in church or other group prayer as fortress, shield, king, friend, lord, shepherd, savior and so on. These images are visual; they offer a picture. In personal prayer, some people do not use visual images, but rather feel or sense a presence. For instance, some pray sensing God as light, love, presence, or a kind of energy field which encompasses them and all of creation. These are "sensed" images.

If our felt image of God is gender-neutral, the emotional sense of God is usually still male because this has been ingrained since childhood. If this is agreeable, fine. But if you are looking for a feminine or truly gender-neutral image, you will need to experiment a bit.

I recommend that, before each meditation, you consciously choose—or let rise within you—some image of God, visual or sensed. Later, reflect on your prayer in relation to that image. Try a different image with the same prayer on another day and see if your prayer or sense of God is any different.

Because of the importance of images, I am taking the liberty of removing any gender-exclusive language for God. God will be "God" and neither masculine nor feminine pronouns will be used. That will offer a wider choice. Of course, you also have the choice of substituting another name for God: Higher Power, The One Who Is, The One Who Is Within, Embracing Spirit and so on.

Knowing God's Love

We want to know God's love in the biblical sense of the word *knowing*. To *know* goes beyond mental recognition and belief. To *know* is to experience. We cannot obtain this kind of knowing, but we can open ourselves to it as gift. Taking a few minutes each day with these meditations is a way of opening ourselves. The words of Paul bless us:

> I pray that you will grasp the breadth and length, the height and depth of Christ's love. I hope you will experience this love which surpasses all knowledge, so that you may enter into the fullness of God (Ephesians 3:18-19).

I Am Chosen by God

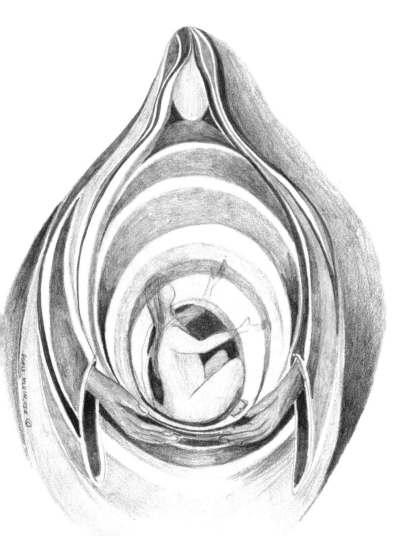

1   Come with me to a quiet place all by yourself
     and rest for a while.

—Mark 6:30

Come away from your work, your family, your
homemaking, your ministry, your friends. Even
more, come away from your fears and your worries, your roles and your masks, your planning and
doing.

Jesus is inviting you to come away to rest in
God's love for some time each day. The gifts God
will give to you in prayer will touch the rest of your
day with the special peace that only God can give.

Come away for a special time to be aware of
God, to experience God, to come to know how
much you are loved. Consider whether you can
reserve five minutes, twenty minutes, or an hour a
day for this and plan when you will do so.

This book offers suggestions for whatever
period of time for prayer you choose.

For Your Day: I will rest with you.

❖ ❖ ❖ ❖ ❖

2   We have varieties of gifts, but the same
     Spirit; and we have varieties of services, but
     the same God.

—1 Corinthians 12:4-5

I hadn't seen five-year-old Hannah in eight
months. "Hey, Hannah," I greeted her, "you surely
are growing up pretty, aren't you?" She charmed

me with a shy smile and a nod. I was pleased. Unfortunately, she probably won't respond so honestly a few years from now.

We all have gifts. Why do we find it so much easier to deny them and to name our faults or failures instead? ("Thank you for saying that, but I didn't do a good job at all with the inside seams.") Are we afraid of pride? of boasting? Are we so caught in the clouds of our shortcomings that they fog our awareness of our skills? Why do we dismiss our gifts with, "Oh well, that's just natural," or, "Oh, that's nothing to speak about."

We brighten other people's lives and our own every day—when we offer hospitality of home or heart, listen even when we are tired, fix an electrical or plumbing problem, or handle a coworker's peevishness effectively. We enrich another when we buy a thoughtful gift, give a loaf of bread, nurture a plant for someone, or touch in a caring way.

You abound in talents, abilities, and skills. Which gifts of yours enrich you and the lives of those around you? Write them down so that you can look at the words and feel the truth. Reflect on how you reveal God's goodness and love through these gifts.

For Your Day: Thank you for my special gifts of
_____.

❖ ❖ ❖ ❖ ❖

3   I taught you to walk,
         I held you in my arms.

                                        —Hosea 11:3

Perhaps you still have an old photo someone took
when you were learning to walk. We get so excited
when a baby takes its first steps. As each of us grew
from infants to toddlers, adults coaxed us into
walking, picked us up from the floor, kissed our
knees and foreheads, and dusted us off. Just so did
God hold out arms and urge us along as we began
to walk in goodness: as we began to give and
receive affection, learned to share, learned to say
no and to care for ourselves, learned to love—a
puppy, a sister, a grandfather. God continues to
walk with us and to teach us, to embrace us when
we succeed and pick us up when we fail.

Before you meet anyone today, think of
God/Jesus walking along with you, ready to help
you bring goodness into this relationship or situation, ready to pick you up if you fail.

For Your Day: I know you are with me.

❖ ❖ ❖ ❖ ❖

4   I pray that you will grasp the breadth and
         length, the height and depth of Christ's love.
         I hope you will experience this love which
         surpasses all knowledge, so that you may
         enter into the fullness of God.

                                        —Ephesians 3:18-19

In his book *Exploring Spiritual Direction*, Alan Jones writes, "The most difficult thing in mature believing is to accept that I am an object of God's delight." We all have some resistance to taking in God's limitless love for us. If we did, would we feel more vulnerable? Would we feel out of control in our relationship with God? Would we feel burdened by such a great gift because we are unable to reciprocate? Do we feel our unworthiness is greater than God's love?

Do you have any idea why you do not relax fully in God's love? Write down any reasons that surface. Take them to Christ, shred them into pieces before him. Accept his delight in you. Go to God and accept God's delight that you are willing to receive love more fully.

For Your Day: I will live in your love.

❖ ❖ ❖ ❖ ❖

5   Do you not know that you are God's temple, and that God's Spirit dwells in you? God's temple is holy, and you are that temple.
              —1 Corinthians 3:16, 17

We are dwelling places, temples for God's Spirit. This passage reveals that we are holy temples. But we suffer assault—sometimes early in life, sometimes later. Even Jesus, the most exquisite house of God, endured assault. The same power that brought Jesus to new life, that "raised the temple in three days," will rebuild us with great beauty.

If you are suffering assault or are afflicted right now, remember that the Spirit of God dwells in you, that you are holy and precious to God. If you are not afflicted at present, recall a time when you were. Were you eventually raised up and made whole? Had you called upon God's Spirit within you?

For Your Day: I am a dwelling place of God.

6 Look, I have inscribed your name on the palms of my hands; I see you continually before me.

—Isaiah 49:16

In biblical times the name of the household owner was burned into his slave's hand. This passage reveals an extraordinary metaphor for God: God as slave. God bears your name. You are the owner of the household. God is like the slave who stands and waits to serve you. Your name is burned into the hand of God.

God's readiness to help strains credibility. Can God love so much? Does God care in such a way? Is God obligated to me?

Picture the coming day and all you will be doing. Consider the faithfulness of your God who stands by you, ready to serve your best interests continually. Anticipate those situations where you especially want to feel God's presence.

For Your Day: I live in your presence.

7   Listen, I am standing at your door and
     knocking. If you can hear me, open the door
     so I can come in and eat dinner with you.
                              —Revelation 3:20

An old picture shows Jesus in a long robe knocking
on a door that has no handle. Only the person on
the other side can open the door to let Jesus in.
Jesus wants to enter, not as master to servant, not
as adult to child, not even as guest to hostess, but
as friend to friend, loved one to loved one.

Do you hesitate about opening the door? If so,
what hinders you? Open it anyway with your
hindrance in your hands. Hold it out to Jesus. If
you are ready to open the door, do so and lead
Jesus into your kitchen or dining room. Sit and chat
awhile.

Plan ahead for some moments today when you
will stop for a chat with Jesus or God.

For Your Day: Thanks for inviting me to spend time
with you.

❖ ❖ ❖ ❖ ❖

8   Our tender and merciful God
         will send the light of dawn to break
         upon you.
     God will give you light
         even when you sit in the shadow of death.
     God will guide your feet on the path of
         peace.
                              —Luke 1:78

God's peace can break through the bleakest of circumstances, even into those moments when we stare into darkness and the shadow of death. A flood of light startles us as it breaks through, the "dawn from on high." By the "tender mercy of our God" we find our feet once paralyzed by fear now flexible again and walking nimbly "on the path of peace." The potential violence of darkness and death yields to the gentle, nonviolent ways of God's dawning light.

Consider a time when you sank into darkness and lived in the shadow of some form of death. Did God's tender mercy touch you then? If so, how? Recall this time and relive it in your imagination, feel the light of the dawn breaking through.

If you are presently feeling darkness or the threat of some form of death, imagine the dawn's light around you and call upon God's promise of tender mercy.

If you have never experienced such darkness or death, give praise for the tender mercy of God in your life.

For Your Day: Write a one-line prayer that reflects your present situation.

9   As the bridegroom rejoices in his bride,
your God rejoices in you.
—Isaiah 62:5

The message is simple, straightforward, powerful, and hard to believe. When someone offers a compliment, we often think, "But if he knew what I was really like." Or when another expresses affection, we say to ourselves, "I wonder what she'd say if she knew . . . about me." We do not trust that others could glimpse our truest and deepest selves and still affirm us. Because we do not love all of who we are, we don't believe that others can or will either.

In this passage consider that the *only* one who knows everything about you not only loves you with the delight of a bridegroom loving his bride, but rejoices in you. Choose an image of God for your prayer and accept God—through that image—rejoicing over you. If negatives about any parts of yourself or your life come to mind, let God especially rejoice over these.

For Your Day: God rejoices in me.

❖ ❖ ❖ ❖ ❖

10   You are precious in my eyes. I honor you and love you.

—Isaiah 43:4

In *Seasons of Your Heart*, Macrina Wiederkehr offers us her poem-prayer called "A Prayer to Own Your Beauty":

O God
help me
to believe

the truth about myself
no matter
how beautiful it is!

To believe the truth is to see ourselves as God sees us, precious and honored, lovable and loved.

In stillness, let the words *precious*, *honored* and *I love you*, as said to you by God, sink into your being.

For Your Day: Pray the poem-prayer above.

❖ ❖ ❖ ❖ ❖

11

I make your name known to them so that the love with which you have loved me may be in them, and I in them.
—John 18:26

At the Last Supper Jesus explained to the disciples and to us one of the reasons for his mission: "that the love with which you have loved me may be in them, and I in them." Among those present were Peter who would deny him, Judas who would betray him, some who were greedy for power or prestige in his kingdom, and others who just didn't understand much of what he had been saying all these years. None of this destroys Jesus' confidence that God's love for them is as great as God's love for himself. None of this keeps Jesus from wanting to be united in love with them.

So what about you and me? Imagine yourself at the Last Supper and listen to Jesus make this statement to Peter, then to Judas, then to those who wanted to sit at his right and left hand in the kingdom, then to those too slow to understand. Then imagine Jesus looking directly at you and making this statement to you. What is your response?

For Your Day: I believe that you love me.

❖ ❖ ❖ ❖ ❖

12   God decides the number of the stars
         And gives all of them their names.
                    —Psalm 147:4

Thinking of a God who knows all the stars by name, monitors the movement of each neuron in the cosmos, smiles at every bird that flies on our planet, and counts the number of hairs on our heads can be overwhelming—especially if we image God as separate from us and creation. We can conceive, however, of a God who expresses himself/herself in all that is created. If everything is an expression of God, a word of God, then God lives in a profound union of intimacy with everything and everyone.

Since you are an expression of God, a word of God constantly being spoken, consider God's union with you. As you think ahead about what you will be saying and doing for the next few hours, sense God's presence in everything. As you end this prayer time to begin other things, hear God whispering your name and saying, "I am within you."

Look at the stars tonight—or imagine a sky full of stars. Give yourself a place among the stars and hear God call you by name.

For Your Day: Hear God saying within you: "I am with you, _____(name)_____."

❖ ❖ ❖ ❖ ❖

13 Now when Jesus entered the area of Caesarea Philippi, he asked his disciples, "Who do people say that the Son of Man is?"

They replied, "Some say John the Baptist, others Elijah, and still others Jeremiah or one of the prophets." He asked them, "But who do you say that I am?"

—Matthew 16:13-15

Like Jesus, we wonder what other people think of us. We would like to know how our family members see us. Our friends. Maybe, if we are brave, our enemies. Yet while we may want to know, we are usually afraid to ask. What we hear may not match our fragile self-image; it may even contradict it. If our self-image is shattered, what will we have, who will we be?

In this passage Peter answers Jesus: "You are the Messiah, the Son of the living God." Jesus confirms that, indeed, he is.

Just as Jesus knew who he was, so God wants us also to know who we are. To do so, we need to give up some parts of our self-image and see ourselves as we are. No part of us, no feeling, is unlovable to God. So we can look at all the parts of ourselves and lovingly receive each. What part of yourself do you find hardest to love? See or hear God loving that part of you. Draw or verbally express your love for that part of yourself even if you don't feel it.

For Your Day: I am a daughter of the living God.

❖ ❖ ❖ ❖ ❖

14   Do not be afraid _____*(your name)*_____ .
I have chosen you.
I will pour out water on the thirsty soul,
And streams on the dry earth.
                              —Isaiah 44:2-4

For what do you thirst? For friendship, forgiveness, appreciation, intimacy, self-esteem, prayerfulness, playfulness, peace? What is it that makes you dry and thirsty? Shame, bitterness, fear, self-rejection, resentments?

You cannot slake your own deepest thirst. But listen with anticipation to God's promise to *pour* water on you.

When you name your own dryness and that for which you thirst, read the passage over and over and hear its message to you. Hold up your hands as a sign of receiving the water. Then trace a path for the streams.

For Your Day: I thirst.

❖ ❖ ❖ ❖ ❖

15
Can a mother forget her baby?
Could she lack tenderness for the child
    of her womb?
Even if she should forget,
I will never forget you.

—Isaiah 49:15,

When the prophet searched for the most tenacious bond and most powerful expression of love to use as a comparison for God's love for us, he chose the love of a woman for her infant. He chose a feminine image of God. We flow from that divine feminine. Our very inner selves are made in that image.

Our culture labels some human qualities as "masculine" or "feminine" even though we recognize that both men and women have these qualities. Consider two of your "feminine" qualities, ones that you most like about yourself. Remember ways in which you exercise them.

For Your Day: I am a woman, an image of my God.

❖ ❖ ❖ ❖ ❖

16
I led you with reins of human kindness,
    with bands of love.
I was like those who lift babies to
    their cheeks.
I bent down to you and gave you your food.

—Hosea 11:4

Many psychologists say that our psychological strength or lack of it may be related to the quality of our early mothering. God assures us of the mothering love she gave and continues to give each of us, regardless of what we received from our birth mothers. We have more power than we think we do. We are stronger than we imagine. God is mothering us continually.

Perhaps we received God's love through the excellent nurturing of our birth or adoptive mothers. Or perhaps neither was available to us. Either way, let's claim our God-parenting strength to go forward. Let's claim the power needed to parent others—our own children, students, our spouse, friends, and co-workers. Let's claim our strength to be good parents to ourselves, for we all continue to need parenting occasionally.

Stand and become aware of your body, legs, and feet as connected to the earth. Spend some minutes recognizing and feeling your own physical and psychological strength rooted in the earth.

For Your Day: Your nurturing strengthens me.

❖ ❖ ❖ ❖ ❖

17   All that happens to us works together for our good as we love God and respond to God's call and purpose.

—Romans 8:28

A mother whose sixteen-year-old daughter was killed by a drunken driver founded MADD (Mothers Against Drunk Driving). Physicist Stephen Hawking said he would not have focused on his work, making such great discoveries and evolving insightful theories, had he not had to combat a progressively crippling sclerosis.

We certainly could not describe all that happens to us as good. Nor do we always "do" good. Life may feel like a garbage dump at times. Yet we are creative persons, flowing from a creative God. With God's power within us, we can use our ashes, tears, charred bricks, and broken glass to rebuild our lives, to turn even the worst of evils into good. God promises it. We can cooperate creatively to do it.

When have you turned something hurtful, sad, or devastating toward some good? How have you changed, matured, or grown in compassion or love as you worked through the grief, anger, and fear in your life?

For Your Day: All that happens to me can work for good.

❖ ❖ ❖ ❖ ❖

18   You formed all the inner parts of my body.
You knit them together while I was in my
        mother's womb.
Thank you for making me so wonderful.
                    —Psalm 139: 13-14

Our local women's theater group wrote and produced a wonderful play called *No Body's Perfect*. With wit and humor, they seriously assailed society's judgments and expectations about women's bodies. Are your thighs too thick? Your hips too large? Your breasts too small? Your nose too crooked? Your complexion too wrinkled?

The play was a hit. We all need an antidote for the poisonous negatives that bombard us. We are targets for the arrows of those with quivers full of products for reducing, de-wrinkling, hi-lighting, and covering.

The psalmist tells you that God made each part of you wonderful (or *awesome* as present usage goes). Although you are not perfect, you are terrific. When have you last praised God for how wonderful you are?

Let yourself be conscious, one by one, of various parts of your body. Give thanks for each part. Reject any of society's critical thoughts that may emerge.

For Your Day: Thank you for making me so wonderful.

❖ ❖ ❖ ❖ ❖

19   The lowly will find joy in God.
                    —Isaiah 29:19

Even though we sometimes feel quite low about ourselves, we don't especially like to label ourselves as "lowly." Emphasizing our lowliness doesn't appear helpful for developing confidence, assertiveness, or self-esteem.

We call ourselves lowly in a healthy way when we recognize that the source of all our confidence, strength, and esteem is God. We know that the springs of life within us are connected to a bottomless reservoir. We can, as Paul says, do all things in

God who strengthens us (2 Corinthians 12:10).

Many refuse to acknowledge the lowliness of their dependence on God. When we do, however, accept our dependence, we know the power of God within us and we find joy.

Remember a time when you felt within yourself a strength or wisdom beyond your own powers. Relive this time and let your awe of God's power, your recognition of your lowliness, again take over in you. If you have not had this experience, ask God to give it to you.

For Your Day: Your power in me brings me joy.

❖ ❖ ❖ ❖ ❖

20   You are a glorious crown of beauty
            in the hand of God,
        a royal diadem held lovingly,
            for your God rejoices in you.
                              —Isaiah 62:3-4

Michelle can be patient with her preschoolers Sarah and Braddon thirty times a day before she yells or punishes. But Michelle will tell you she is impatient. Kristine has a good driving record, but, after two traffic mistakes in one afternoon, she is on her own case over what a poor driver she is becoming.

Many of us are overly hard on ourselves. We do not value our virtues, our talents, our skills, our capacity to love. We find it hard to receive compliments. We hesitate to go forward for fear of failure.

Sometimes we don't even trust our friends who tell us our good qualities.

But God delights in us as in a crown of great beauty. If we can safely assume that God has good taste, we have every reason to delight in ourselves.

Have you ever seen a crown of jewels? Even those set with imitation stones can be dazzling. Genuine ones inspire awe. Often a crown itself is a work of art. Consider the crown that you are and the jewels that you have. Write down the names of some of your jewels; for instance, skills you have, the kinds of things you do for others, your personality qualities that help you relate to others. Consider especially what you do daily. Draw or paint them on a crown to be nestled in the hand of God.

For Your Day: You rejoice in me; I will rejoice in myself today.

❖ ❖ ❖ ❖ ❖

21
My soul is a mirror of God
    my spirit rejoices in God, my Savior.
God has looked with favor on my lowliness.
Surely from now on, generations will call
    me blessed.
God has done great things in me;
    holy is God's name.
—Luke 1:46-49

Mary was a woman who knew who she was. When someone praised her, she did not say, "I really didn't do too much," or, "I only did what I was supposed to do," or any of the other cliches with which we diffuse a compliment. Mary understood her place of lowliness in the social scale, yet acknowledged the greatness of all that was happening in her. She knew that all things were possible through God's power and her cooperation.

God has done and is doing great things in *you*. Acknowledge this. Consider the great things that are the results of your love, your care, your talents, efforts, and cooperation. Look at the great everyday things you are doing such as providing a warm or beautiful space for living, sending a casserole or deli tray to the family down the street with the newborn set of twins, listening empathetically to a coworker suffering the breakup of a relationship, getting old friends together for support and comfort or fun, inviting a lonely person for a meal, helping a colleague gain some needed information, taking good care of the body you are given, parenting a child through another crisis, praying for an end to a standoff in the extended family. Greatness is in the "lowly" daily things.

For Your Day: God is doing great things in me. Holy is God's name.

God Promises Good to Me

22   I will bring you home.
      —Zephaniah 3:20

Some of us call home the place where we live, or the place of our childhood. Some call home an eternal place with God. Going home may also be a return to one's genuine self, an acceptance of one's gifts and limitations, one's beauty and brokenness. God wants to bring us home from the exile of pretending, of putting up defensive fronts before others. God wants to relieve us of the burden of wearing excess clothing and styles that are not of our native country.

Coming home to ourselves means discovering and accepting everything about ourselves. We may even have covered up attractive qualities like gentleness, assertiveness, or tears of vulnerability, thinking that they are not acceptable. We must uncover all the ways that God has made us and claim them as treasures.

When God brings you home to yourself, what gifts and beautiful qualities do you suspect will be uncovered there?

What gifts of God within yourself do you sometimes see as liabilities—your anger, desires, feelings of irritation, quietness, ability to speak your mind?

Plan four or five times today when you will stop and think of a gift or beautiful quality that you have. Name a different one each time. Ask God to bring you home.

For Your Day: Bring me home.

❖ ❖ ❖ ❖ ❖

23   I know what plans I have in mind for you,
plans for your good, not for harm, offering a
future full of hope for you.

—Jeremiah 29:11

Inevitably the question: If God loves me so much
and has only good plans for me, why am I suffering
such-and-such in my life? Why did such-and-such
a tragedy happen?

Consider that while God only wants what is for
our good, God does not take away the freedom of
others who may obstruct the good in mind for us.
God does not take away our freedom to make
unwise choices. God does not change the workings
of the universe in which natural calamities occur.
Yet God is with us, willing our good, working out
good even from evil. God is within us and in those
around us who are also open to the good.

Ask God for the Spirit of Wisdom. Ask for insight and courage to make wise choices, to be
aware of God's presence and love helping you to
turn suffering into good.

For Your Day: Give me wisdom.

❖ ❖ ❖ ❖ ❖

24   Even to your old age I am your God.
Even when your hair turns gray,
    I will carry you.

> I have always supported you, and I
>   will continue.
> I will carry you to safety.
>   —Isaiah 46:4

When we reluctantly look at our wrinkles in the mirror, when our muscles ache more than they used to after planting the garden, when the optician smiles and advises trifocals, God just watches us with love (and maybe a little amusement?). When gray streaks our hair and the battle of the bulge becomes a losing one, God carries us in steady arms.

Does anyone else reflect to you this total faithfulness of God? If so, dwell for a few minutes in the love of this person. Then dwell in God's love coming through that person.

If not, spend as much time as you can today letting God's loving care surround you. Relax in it. Trust in it. Reread the words of the verse and let them fill you.

For Your Day: Repeat the promise, "Even when your hair turns gray I will carry you."

❖ ❖ ❖ ❖ ❖

25   A Samaritan woman came to the well to draw water, and Jesus spoke to her: "Give me a drink." The Samaritan woman replied, "How can you, a Jew, ask for a drink from me, a woman of Samaria?" Jesus said, "If you knew the gift of God, and who I am, asking you to give me a drink, you would

>have asked him, and he would have given
>you living water."
>
>—John 4:7-10

Read the complete story if you can. If time is short today, reread the selection above. In either case, *be* the Samaritan woman as you read it. Would you ask for the living water?

If not, what keeps you from asking?

If yes, what does living water mean to you? The experience of God's presence? Eternal life? Strength? Wisdom? Intimacy with God or Jesus? Forgiveness? Ability to forgive?

Imagine yourself at the well with Jesus asking for the living water you want. Or imagine yourself in sight of the well and Jesus, but holding back, not yet ready to approach Jesus.

For Your Day: Give me to drink.

❖ ❖ ❖ ❖ ❖

26 Come to me, you who work hard and carry heavy burdens. I will give you rest.
>   —Matthew 11:28

Women around the globe carry heavy water jugs, or baskets of bread or fruit, on their heads. This burden only symbolizes their heavier burden of finding enough food and water each day so that they and their husbands and children do not starve. A heavy burden indeed.

Yet Jesus spoke of even heavier burdens he wishes to lift from them and us. He wants us all to be free from the burden of having nearly every moment governed by law: endless lists of details, the "shoulds" and "oughts" of home, church, school, or society. While elsewhere he affirms the importance of law in general, he assures us that we are not saved through obeying every detail, but, rather, through faith in him. We do not have the burden of earning our freedom or salvation. Jesus removes the basket and jugs from our heads and places them on the table before us.

We are called to sort out the many "oughts" and "shoulds" to see which spring from the gospel and which just burden us with cultural baggage, for example: This is the way it *should* be done when "it" could actually be done in many ways.

Sort out your laws. God wants you to be as free as possible. Listen for at least two "shoulds" or "oughts" today; ask where they come from and whether you want to keep them.

For Your Day: I am weary and seek your rest.

❖ ❖ ❖ ❖ ❖

27 The Spirit will help you when you do not know how to pray as you ought. The Spirit will intercede with prayers too deep for words. God searches hearts and knows the mind of the Spirit who intercedes for everyone according to the will of God.
—Romans 8:26-27

What should we pray for? Should we ask God for the cure of an eighty-two-year-old diabetic woman suffering from pneumonia and a staph infection? Should we pray for the cure of a friend in the last stages of lung cancer? Should we request that someone we love gets that particular job she has her eye on? Should we pray to sell the house quickly? Should we comply with an elderly aunt's request that we ask God to take her soon?

Sometimes we need to pray about what to pray about. At other times, we can let go of those decisions because we have a Spirit within that will intercede according to the will of God. The Spirit gives us freedom to lift up the person we love and give him or her to God.

Consider times when situations worked out differently than you would have prayed for or planned, and yet seemingly worked out for the best.

For Your Day: Holy Spirit, intercede for those I love.

❖ ❖ ❖ ❖ ❖

28   Ask and you will receive; if you seek, you will find; knock and the door will open for you. For those who ask do receive, and those who search do find, and those who knock do have the door opened for them.
—Matthew 7:7

"If Jesus has said that God will give us what we ask for, why have so many of my prayers gone unanswered?" says just about anyone.

The absolute guarantee of the scripture passage is not attached to requests for sunny skies for the picnic, tromping the other team in the tournament, or even getting a raise—important as these may seem at the time. Nor is it fastened onto asking for a return to health for someone we love, the recovery of an addict in the family, or money for a college education—though we certainly are invited to pray for things of such significance.

God fulfills the biblical promise when we ask for the self-transformation we need to serve as disciples (John 15:7-9), when we pray for what will open the door of the reign of God, the reign of love, to ourselves and others. When we seek, we will find within ourselves the gifts of wisdom, compassion, and courage. God responds when we ask about the meaning of our lives and the events in them, our purpose on earth, about who God is, and how God works in our lives. The answers to these prayers give perspective and meaning to the picnic, the tournament, the raise, a recovery, a healing, and our needs for the future.

For what do you most deeply ask, search, and knock at the door? Name it and claim Jesus' promise.

For Your Day: I ask, I seek, I knock.

29 Would any among you give a stone to your child who is asking you for bread? Or if your child asks for fish, will you hand over a poisonous snake? If you then, who can do wrong, give good gifts to your children, don't you think that your Father/Mother in heaven will give you good things when you ask?

—Matthew 7:9-11

Could Jesus have offered us a more convincing analogy? Consider how even the most poverty-stricken of parents, the most dishonest in business, the most revengeful in the neighborhood want to please their children with the gifts they give to them. Even more our all-loving, all-good Parent wants to give us what is for our good.

What gift do you want? A healing of your spirit? Overcoming an addiction or compulsion? Forgiveness? The ability to forgive others? Or to forgive yourself? Knowing the way to follow Jesus more closely? Finding what you can do to bring about a more just world? Wisdom for a life-changing or life-enhancing decision? Freedom from the tyranny of inner criticism? Liberation from those "shoulds" and "oughts"?

Picture God as Mother or Father and yourself as God's (adult) child asking for the gift you want. Notice how much the Parent wants to give it. Watch yourself receive it.

For Your Day: I thank you for the gift of _____
                    (whatever you just requested)   .

30 Take my yoke upon yourself and learn from me. I am gentle and humble of heart and you will find inner rest. My yoke is easy and my burden light.

—Matthew 11:29-30

Jesus' yoke is obedience to God. One way that Jesus lived obedience was by accepting the limitations of being human. His number of years on earth limited him, as did the tiny area of the planet on which he preached, the slowness of his friends and disciples to understand, and his own need for food and rest when he had so much to do in so short a time.

Consider what it is for you to be obedient to God by accepting the needs of your body. Giving yourself balanced meals and adequate rest fulfills part of God's will. For you are loved by the God who made you. Extraordinary circumstances may call you to let go of your needs for a time. In ordinary circumstances, however, you are called to love yourself as God loves you, to give yourself what you need, and to accept your limitations. It is part of taking up the yoke of Jesus, of being obedient to God.

What needs of your body are you especially good at meeting? Giving yourself healthy food? Appropriate amounts of food? Muscle-toning exercise? Sufficient sleep? Time for relaxing? Ways of reducing stress? Care for any weakened parts such as heart, lungs, arthritic limbs?

For Your Day: I will respect the needs of my body.

❖ ❖ ❖ ❖ ❖

31 I am about to create a new heaven and a new earth; former things shall be forgotten. So be happy and rejoice in what I am creating.
—Isaiah 65:17-18

We get excited when trees burst forth into leaves and plants shoot up their heads in spring. We feel energetic warmth when we recognize that someone we care about is growing to greater maturity and love. We wonder "awe-fully" when we look at an intricate pencil sketch, hear a melody that touches our feelings, or walk into a room with a beautifully set dinner table.

God continually creates, constantly develops the world. Wondrously, God takes us into partnership in this creativity. We, too, continually mold our own lives while shaping those around us. We fashion things from the world of nature and evolve even greater beauty from the forms God provides.

Consider the ways you co-create with God to make your spaces and relationships more livable and lovable. Perhaps you do it in furnishing and decorating your living room in a simple or an elegant way, offering warm hospitality, planning and planting a garden, devising a new management plan, cooking and serving a special casserole, or figuring out a better way to support, teach, or heal someone. Being invited to offer a suggestion at work or spearhead a project to build morale are all opportunities to create. So are praying, singing, playing, doing arts and crafts, writing, and talking with others.

What activities in the normal course of your day are creative? How will you be creative today? Plan to recognize your own creativity and rejoice in it.

For Your Day: I will create goodness and beauty today.

❖ ❖ ❖ ❖ ❖

32   Look, I am making all things new.
—Revelation 21:5

All of our body cells replace themselves every seven years. We are physically a new creation. Many of us find this scientific fact as hard to fathom as the mysteries of faith. All of God's ways are full of wonder.

Do we believe that God renews our spirits as well as our bodies? Do we believe that God's Spirit can so fill us that we can unload our hurtful, painful memories and drop them in a trail behind us as we walk on into new life? When we ask for God's reign to come "on earth as it is in heaven," we are asking that those pieces of the earth that are ourselves be created anew.

Consider the following questions and enter into prayer for a minute or two as you answer each one.

How would I like to be created anew?

What kind of newness does God want me to express?

What former things will I need, with God's power, to discard?

Can I rejoice in what God is doing with me?

For Your Day: God is renewing me, body and soul.

❖ ❖ ❖ ❖ ❖

33   [God said to Jacob:] "I will not go away until I have completed what I have promised you." Then Jacob awakened from his sleep and said, "Surely God is here—and I did not know it."

—Genesis 28:15

Even in Jacob's sleep, God renewed the promise of personal faithfulness. Like us, Jacob must have needed reassurance.

God did not chide him, but gave him what he wanted.

God did not stop being present just because Jacob lacked awareness of God. The promise of faithfulness is God's promise to be with us—no matter where we are and what happens.

God is living within you, aware of you right now, and will be with you as you go about your next twenty-four hours. When you stop to pick up milk from the grocery, when you receive a longer telephone call than you want, when you are stuck in traffic behind a construction crew blocking a lane, when one of your children anguishes over a problem, when you scrub the potatoes . . . God is with you. Right now, imagine God with you for the next twenty-four hours—in your tasks, in your leisure, and in your socializing.

For Your Day: Surely God is here.

❖ ❖ ❖ ❖ ❖

34 Ask and you will receive, so that your joy may be full.

—John 16:24

Jesus plainly states that God wants us to have joy. Money and possessions, job success, bodily pleasures, and having charge of one's life do bring a certain, often healthy, joy into our lives. Love, family, and friends bring deeper joy. Yet God's joy, like God's peace, exceeds all of these.

We can enter into God's joy when we are willing to receive God's unconditional love. When we believe that our lives make a difference and accept that we, with all the universe, have meaning, the joy of God leaps up like a flame within us. Then all the joys of our lives glow in this bright light of faith. This flame of joy remains alive even when other lights in our lives grow dim.

When have you experienced the joy of God either undergirding your life or exploding happily for a while in it? What would bring you closer to accepting the joy that God wants to give you? Ask for that gift and claim the promise of John 16:24.

For Your Day: Repeat your petition throughout
the day.

❖ ❖ ❖ ❖ ❖

35   I will place my spirit in you and you will live.
I will put you down on your own soil and
you will know that I, your God, have done
as I have promised.

—Ezekiel 37:14

God places us on the ground of our own intuitive
knowing, places us in the deep recesses where our
knowledge and decisions can be trusted. Here they
are in-spirited with God's spirit. Society teaches us
to trust only fact, logic, and reason. We are just
beginning to stand up and claim our other ways of
knowing and deciding. We need to trust the soil,
the place of power within us, against the overly
rational forces who would dismiss us.

With a certain humility that allows for error on
our part, we need to learn to listen to ourselves *first*,
to test out our intuition rather than to dismiss it as
we have been taught. Recall times when your intuition, your sense of a situation or place or person
has been proven accurate in the long run.

For Your Day: Help me to listen for your Spirit
within me.

❖ ❖ ❖ ❖ ❖

36   In quiet and trust you shall find your
strength.

—Isaiah 30:15

We hunger for quiet times: we find in them a womb to renew our strength. We ache for quiet times to connect with our center. We can also grow restless in the quiet as the shadow of some deep loneliness emerges. We sometimes need to face our loneliness in the strength of God. Either way, quiet is good.

We each have different needs for different kinds and amounts of quiet. How much do you need? Do you get it? If you do, spend some time appreciating this gift and source of strength. If not, consider what you must do to add it to your life.

Think of a place where you can relax and a time to be quiet even for just fifteen or twenty minutes today. Think of a place and time to set aside a half-day or a whole one to just be yourself, to rest and, perhaps, to dream and pray.

For Your Day: You are with me.

❖ ❖ ❖ ❖ ❖

37   Your God is a God of justice;
Blessed are those who wait for God.
—Isaiah 30:18

The mention of God's justice sparks fear. Just the word can wisk some of us back to our childhood image of a thunderbolt God, or the muscular God of judgment in Michelangelo's painting on the ceiling of the Sistine Chapel. Thérèse of Lisieux, however, wrote that she felt comforted more by thinking of God's justice than of God's mercy. In justice, she says, God has to take into account our human nature, the weaknesses inherent in us, and all that makes us what and who we are. Justice, she believes, will put any judgment in our favor.

Again we wait for God's justice. Isaiah persuades us that those who do so are blessed, happy. God's justice, unlike many of the judgments of human beings, is to be welcomed. Spend some time today consciously waiting for and trusting your God of justice.

For Your Day: I wait for you.

❖ ❖ ❖ ❖ ❖

38   Neither death, nor life, nor angels, nor rulers, nor anything present, nor anything to come, nor powers, nor height, nor depth, nor anything else in creation is able to separate you from the love of God in Christ Jesus.
—Romans 8:38-39

As the world imposes its standards on us and we fail to measure up, we absorb shame. The world tells us to be cool in our emotional responses, independent, successful, part of the "right" crowd, without pain, without fear, knowledgeable, totally competent. Jesus, of course, ignored these standards. He showed his emotions, depended on his friends, went about as an ordinary person, cried out as he suffered, showed fear and often failed to get his message across. Because he chose to live simply, truthfully, and vulnerably instead of trying to meet the world's demands, the world hated him.

For the same reasons, we love him.

Our shame comes from the false teachings of "the world" that tell us it's not all right to be truly human. But we can accept our humanity as Jesus did and then nothing can separate us "from the love of God in Christ Jesus."

Today watch for any subtle feelings of shame about something that merely indicates you are human, i.e. needing affirmation, making mistakes, feeling afraid. Let them go. Jesus says it is all right to be human. You are loved.

For Your Day: Nothing can separate me from your love.

❖ ❖ ❖ ❖ ❖

39 O afflicted one, storm-tossed, and not
    comforted,
I am about to set your stones in antimony,
    and lay your foundations with sapphires.
I will make your pinnacles of rubies,
    and your gates of jewels.
And all your wall of precious stones.
—Isaiah 54:11-12

God promises an end to your sufferings. You will no longer live with the pain of separation, loss, or failure from the past. You will be able to live in the present moment where each encounter, task, or leisure moment will be a jewel.

"Just to be is blessing; just to live is holy," writes Rabbi Abraham Heschel. When afflictions, confusion, and loneliness have passed, you will value the present and become aware of its great treasures. You are a treasure of the present.

Consider some of the treasures you will experience in the coming day and let yourself be aware of them.

For Your Day: Today is a treasure chest of jewels.

❖ ❖ ❖ ❖ ❖

40   Do not worry about your life, about what you will eat, or about your body and what you will wear. For life is more important than food, your body more important than clothing. Consider the birds who neither sow nor reap, they have neither cellars nor barns, and God feeds them. How much more valuable you are than the birds!
—Luke 12:22-24

Count inner freedom among God's great gifts. Jesus says we can have this gift if we are willing to give up something for it: worrying. We can give up worrying if we trust someone who cares for us— God. Jesus gives us the assurance of this care.

Some graced, happy people have discovered that freedom from worry is a far greater gift than money, travel, a luxurious home, or elegant clothes. This gift is offered to us all.

Of course, Jesus didn't tell us to forget about planning to provide for ourselves and others. He said to do so without worry. Can you identify your worries?

For Your Day: Whenever you feel drawn to worry today, let go of the thought. Instead, pray: "I trust in you" or "I place _____ in your hands."

❖ ❖ ❖ ❖ ❖

41   I will go before you,
            leveling the mountains,
        I will shatter the doors of bronze
            and snap the bars of iron.
        I will give you the treasures stored in
            darkness
            and riches hidden in secret places.
                                    —Isaiah 45:2-3

God wants us to know that divine power causes breakthroughs in our life journeys. God wants us to recognize these as acts of love given us as individuals. God calls each of us by name.

By what name or names does God call you? Your baptismal name? Your nickname? A descriptive name such as "Beloved" or "Fearful One" or "Energetic One"? Reread the verse aloud and place one of the names God calls you at the end of the first line and after *you* in the fifth line. Do this again for each name that God calls you.

Hear God say your name or names frequently throughout the day.

For Your Day: I have called you by name _____
                            (your name)   .

God's Love and Faithfulness
Enfold Me

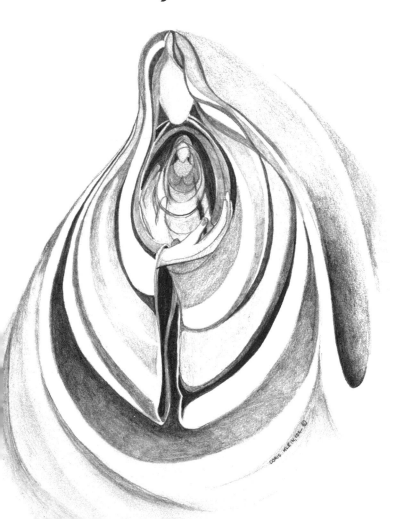

42
> Even if the mountains should leave
>   their place
>   and the hills be shaken,
> My love will never leave you.
> —Isaiah 54:10

Is there anything we want more than to feel fully loved just as we are? Yet, as we hear the Good News that such an all-encompassing love is ours, we stumble backwards in disbelief. Even when the Spirit of God assures us that we are already filled with this gift, we are afraid to trust it. Is it God whom we mistrust? Or ourselves?

Repeat aloud several times the verse from Isaiah. Say your own name at the beginning when you repeat the verse for the first few times. Then say your name at the end. Try saying it before the last line. Hear the words spoken by God to you.

As you begin the meditations of this section, ask that you may accept and *experience* more of the total love God has for you. Ask for this gift often today.

For Your Day: I open my heart to receive your love.

❖ ❖ ❖ ❖ ❖

43
> Martha, Martha, you are distracted and worried about so many things, but only one thing is necessary. Mary has chosen the better part, and it will not be taken away from her.
> —Luke 10:41

Many women hate the story of Mary and Martha. Most of us are Marthas, and we resent the "correction" for being faithful to our duties.

Let's set one thing straight. Jesus loved Martha deeply. It was Martha who ran to meet Jesus on the road after Lazarus died and it was to Martha that Jesus announced, "I am the resurrection and the life." When Jesus asked her, "Do you believe this?" Martha made one of the greatest acts of faith recorded in scripture: "Yes, Lord, I believe that you are the Messiah, the Son of God, the one coming into the world" (John 11:25-27).

Knowing how much Jesus loved Martha, let's go back to his "correction." Jesus didn't tell her that she should stop working or serving. Rather, he invited her to get her work and service in better perspective. He asked her not to be so worried and distracted by it that she wasn't able to just spend some time with him. (He obviously wanted to spend more time with her.) Jesus offered Martha greater freedom, freedom to do what she wanted to do anyway: just sit and talk with her friend Jesus.

Invite Jesus to your home and imagine how you would prepare. How would you greet him and serve him? In his unique love for you, might Jesus call you to any greater freedom?

For Your Day: I center on you today, as I do what I need to do.

❖ ❖ ❖ ❖ ❖

44   Live wisely.
                    —Ephesians 5:15

As women, as human beings, we are lovers. We must love not only well, but wisely. We love our families and friends, the earth and its creatures. We work to promote harmony, peace, and justice. In trying to do so, we sometimes burn out or emotionally dry up. We can go on no longer. Songwriter Carolyn McDade says, "No woman is required to build the world by destroying herself."

Most of us need to learn to love others and ourselves *wisely*. While some extraordinary circumstance may require the sacrifice of our lives or our temporary well-being, we need to lay down our lives on a day to day basis with balance and harmony, showing toward our own body and spirits the peace and justice we would like others to experience.

For Your Day: Help me to live and love wisely.

❖ ❖ ❖ ❖ ❖

45   I will praise the God of our Lord Jesus Christ who has given me every spiritual blessing in Christ.

                    —Ephesians 1:3

On Holy Saturday, we sang eight verses of "I Have Loved You With an Everlasting Love" as we waited for the newly baptized to return to the church. We had baptized them by immersion and promised eighteen-year-old Sharon that she could dry her hair before she emerged again from the sacristy.

Looking at her rosy, embarrassed face as she and the four others processed back into the church, I asked myself how Sharon was different since her baptism. Paul tells us that now Sharon, like us, has every spiritual blessing. We are not, however, always aware of our blessings. For Sharon and us, God's gifts become active in our lives only when we receive and recognize them.

Each of us has already accepted some of the gifts, perhaps hope, or peace, or a sense of God's presence in nature. Maybe we have been afraid of some of the others such as courage, or patience, or long-suffering because of what they demand of us.

Follow the old adage, "Count your blessings." Which of God's blessings are a cause for rejoicing or gratitude in your life so far? Consider especially the spiritual ones.

For Your Day: Thank you for my many blessings.

❖ ❖ ❖ ❖ ❖

46   In God we live and move and exist.
                    —Acts 17:28

Some mystics say that we find God when we find our deepest selves. But society does not want us to find our true selves. Our culture wants us to live and move and take our being from it. Quite early, quite clearly, it asks that we take on roles, serve its needs, and follow its current model for the "ideal woman." To live in God means instead to listen to the inner voice of the deepest self and to risk society's criticisms.

Let the verse from Acts reassure you that you and God are inexplicably bound as one. God is more one with you than are your heart or your brain. Your very person is an expression of God. You are a daughter, enveloped and suffused in God's love where you live and move and have your being.

Consider your need to trust yourself as you discover more and more of your true self within. Consider the courage it takes to act from within, especially when it may be at variance with what others, even religious people, may say. Obedience means listening. Consider what obedience means when you apply it to listening to your true self, a word of God living in God.

For Your Day: In you I live.

❖ ❖ ❖ ❖ ❖

47   Aren't two sparrows sold for only a penny? Still, not one of them falls to the ground without God knowing it. Even the hairs of your head are all counted. So, don't be afraid; you are more valuable than many sparrows.

—Matthew 10:29-30

Lots of sparrows fall to the ground from hunger, cold, or attack. Jesus did not say that they wouldn't. Only that no sparrows would fall without God's knowledge. Our God has never promised that we would escape suffering or that only good things would happen to us. Everyone gets turned on the wheel of sorrow. Jesus, however, tells us the Good News that God's presence and love are greater than whatever happens to us. When we know and trust in this personal love for us we can walk unafraid.

God is so intimate as to know the number of hairs on your head. So consider what God knows about each of your concerns. Yet, you are commanded, "Do not be afraid."

Imagine a pile of feathers in front of you. Place each of your concerns on one of them and blow them away from you in different directions.

For Your Day: I live in your care.

❖ ❖ ❖ ❖ ❖

48   If God is for you, who is against you?
—Romans 8:31

Who are those who seem to be against us? Persons who want us to be other than we are? Persons who want to use us for their own advantage? Persons who are jealous and want to lower us in the eyes of others? Persons who treat us angrily and won't say why? Persons who ignore our opinions?

We are chosen by one who wants us to become fully who we are; who works within us for our own good as well as that of others; who loves us actively and aggressively; who calls us to be one in his/her divinity.

Visualize someone whom you feel is or has been against you. Visualize God protecting you with a shield of esteem and love against the negative arrows of the other.

For Your Day: If you are for me, who can be against me?

❖ ❖ ❖ ❖ ❖

49   God has given you all things—the earth, life, death, the present, the future. They all belong to you. And you belong to Christ and Christ is God's.

—1 Corinthians 3:21-23

I walked with my three-year-old twin nephews in a crowded garden center. Dan and I had a firm grip on each other's hand. David came from behind where he had been admiring a bird-of-paradise and said in a stage-whisper loud enough for others to hear, "I want a hand, too." Smiles and "ahs" of empathy surrounded us.

Each of us feels the need of belonging—to someone, some group, or perhaps some cause larger than ourselves. Belonging overcomes aloneness and helps us to transcend ourselves, to let go of some of our false ego.

Paul tells us that we are one with everything and

everyone. Can we belong more fully than that? Yes! We belong to Christ and Christ to God. We are one with the God within us and the God who fills the universe, as well as with the universe itself.

God and everything in the world belong to us. Yet, at times, each of us asks: Why do I feel so separate, so out-of-it? Why do I often feel my lack of connection more than my unity? How can I take the separated puzzle pieces of my world and bring them together into the picture of unity which is the deeper truth?

Talk to God about your own questions or about what becomes yours in Christ. Ask God to take your hand.

For Your Day: All things are mine.

❖ ❖ ❖ ❖ ❖

50   Consider the love God has given you, that you are called a daughter of God. Indeed, that is what you are.

—1 John 3:1

You are a daughter of God the Father, God the Mother. Some of us had good parenting from loving, though imperfect, human parents. Some us had inadequate or abusive parenting. Some of us had only one parent or a parent substitute on the scene.

In God we have the all-loving, all-wise Mother and Father.

Can you imagine yourself in some way being born of God the Mother, the Father? Can you picture yourself flowing from God, being an expression of God as is any child of its parents? Imagine yourself enveloped in a radiance of love as you come forth. Feel God's embrace, God's caring, God's nurturing as you grow.

What you are imaging is true. In whatever has happened and is happening, your Mother/Father's unconditional love surrounds you. Although God did not interrupt the gift of free will and stop whatever criticism, neglect, or abuse may have happened early in your life, God never stopped loving you or working toward healing in you. God is still doing so, or you wouldn't be praying this today.

If your parents reflected God's love beautifully, give thanks to them and to God. If your parents were not able to do that, spend some more time imaging yourself being birthed and nurtured by God.

For Your Day: I am God's daughter.

❖ ❖ ❖ ❖ ❖

51   Why are you still afraid? Have you no faith?
—Mark 4:40

A cartoon by Betty Woods shows two eagles flying high. One is struggling to keep on flying with a full tree trunk in its claws. The companion is calling "You've got to learn to let go."

We can create problems by trying to exercise too much control. Do I, perhaps, over-control my inner responses so that neither I nor others can know what I feel? Do I try to control my spouse, my children, my friends, my boss or employees? Or do I excel at controlling events, planning everything in such minute detail that nothing can go wrong—except that no one enjoys the experience because they feel choked by my planning?

We control because we are afraid. We are trying to avoid being hurt or rejected if we ask directly for what we want or need. We are afraid of being seen as less than perfect and therefore not lovable. Jesus tells us to let go, to turn our fears over to him and to live more freely. This is what faith is all about.

Think about the controls and fears from which Jesus wants to release you. Today is the day to watch for them in yourself, to be aware of what keeps you from living more joyfully. Today is a day to let go.

Lie down on the floor and hold your arms out spread-eagle to express your vulnerability and desire not to control.

For Your Day: Teach me to let go and trust in you.

52   I tell you all this so that you may be filled with my joy.

—John 17:13

What does Jesus care about? Our joy. That our joy be as complete as his. How can we have joy when our world cries out in suffering? How could Jesus have joy? People walked away from him or tried to trip him up. His best friend denied him and another of his close circle betrayed him to killers. Other friends didn't understand and fell asleep while he suffered. Political leaders had him scourged and, at the request of his religious leaders, put him to death. Is this *joy*?

Obviously Jesus' joy is a different kind and has a deeper quality than the "world's." He wants us to have it. Completely.

Stand up and recall several major world problems and several problems in your own life. Face in a different direction for each one. Then imagine the crucified Jesus near you. Ask him about his joy even in the midst of problems and suffering. Ask if he has anything to tell you.

For Your Day: I want to know your joy.

❖ ❖ ❖ ❖ ❖

53   I have loved you as God has loved me.
—John 15:9

Friendship is the warm cloak we wear over our winter lives. Friends wrap us with affirmation, enfold us with understanding, and protect us against the cold winds of hostility and criticism.

Friendship is the cool breeze of our summer lives. Friends sail along with us in our pleasure, enjoy the sun of our successes, and breathe care-fulness upon us.

God's loving friendship clasps Jesus so closely that they are one with each other. Jesus asks for such a friendship with us. Even if we have never experienced a close friendship with another human being, God offers us a total experience.

Think about your closest friend, what you receive and give. For a few minutes, remain in the sunshine of your friend's acceptance. In what ways is Jesus' friendship like this one? In what ways is it more? Pray for a few minutes to Jesus about what he wants for you.

If you do not have such a close friend, imagine what having one would be like. Then know that Jesus is offering you even more. What might you expect from Jesus' friendship?

For Your Day: I walk in your friendship.

❖ ❖ ❖ ❖ ❖

54   I pray for the God of our Lord Jesus Christ to give you a spirit of wisdom and clarity as you get to know God. May the eyes of your heart be filled with light so that you may know the hope to which God calls you, the riches of God's glorious inheritance to be shared among the saints.

—Ephesians 1:17-18

First of all, yes, you are among the saints. We've often heard that saints are the sinners who kept on trying. It is not in our deeds, but in God's love for us and call to us that we are made holy. If you were not a saint, you would not be praying this book.

Secondly, yes, this prayer is for you. Reread the passage slowly and underline or jot down what Paul and the church ask for you. Which do you need the most? Which most appeals to you? What is the hope to which you are called?

Remembering all who have read this passage down through the ages, offer this prayer. Pray it now for yourself. Then pray it for someone else. If you belong to a community of Christians, pray it for them.

For Your Day: Enlighten the eyes of my heart.

❖ ❖ ❖ ❖ ❖

55   What do you want me to do for you?
—Mark 10:51

What a wonderful turnabout to have someone ask what we want done for us! We are so used to having others, especially family members, expect us to do for them. Take in these words of Jesus as you type the extra letters, wrap the food to microwave for the next meal, drive someone to the dentist, throw another load in the washer, make the extra phone calls, organize the fund drive, or stay up late to go to the airport.

"What do you want me to do for you?" Give this considerable thought. What do you want from Jesus more than anything else?

If you have time, go slowly through Mark 10:46-52 imagining the whole scene and yourself as the blind person. Hear Jesus say: "What do you want me to do for you?"

For Your Day: Ask Jesus frequently for what you want.

❖ ❖ ❖ ❖ ❖

56   May your love overflow more and more as you keep on growing in knowledge and insight to help you to decide what is best.
　　　　　　　　　—Philippians 1:9-10

"Off with her head," commands the Queen of Hearts in *Alice in Wonderland*. Indeed, how many of us had our heads chopped off quite young! We began living as if we had nothing below the neck—or nothing above it. We blocked our feelings and did what we were "supposed to do," or we let our feelings drive us, paying no attention to our reason. God calls us to integrate our minds and hearts, to let our love overflow with knowledge and insight so that we will do what is best for ourselves and others.

Consider whether your head or your heart have dominated years of your life. Or if either still does. Imagine your mind or your heart as separate from you and carry on a conversation with it. You can do this aloud or on paper. See what your mind or your heart has to say to you.

For Your Day: Help me to know what is best.

57 Everyone who is loving knows God and reflects God.

—1 John 4:7

Babies reflect God. Who hasn't known tiny arms reaching out to embrace and be embraced? All of us were born to love and be loved. But mishandling often diminishes the giving and receiving that is intended to flow freely to us and from us.

God's love, like the sun, shines on us continually even when hurt opens a parasol that keeps it from touching our skin. Our love, too, goes out to others, though sometimes they put up a wall to block its warmth. Even events in our lives may make it hard for us to feel God's love.

We could add to the passage, however, that everyone who desires to love is also born of God, for only God can give this desire. In other passages John says, "God *is* love."

Set aside some time to think of the people whom you love and have loved. Be aware that God *is* love.

Take some additional time to remember all the people who love and have loved you. Be aware that God *is* love.

For Your Day: You and I are one in love.

❖ ❖ ❖ ❖ ❖

58 If a woman loses one of her ten silver coins, doesn't she light a lamp, sweep the house and look carefully for it? When she finds it, she calls her friends and neighbors together saying, "Celebrate with me, for I have found the coin that I lost." Just so is the joy of God and the angels over one sinner who repents.

—Luke 15:8-10

Another parable occurs just before this one in Luke 15. In it a shepherd who has a hundred sheep loses one and goes in search of it. The story of the homemaker searching for a lost coin follows it. Both the shepherd and the homemaker are images of God who searches us out when we get lost. Notice that Jesus uses a man for one image of God and a woman for the other.

Go back over the story and name some of the qualities of the woman. What does Jesus tell us of God through her? Think about imaging God as feminine and how it affects you.

For Your Day: I am her daughter, sister, friend. (Choose one relationship word or repeat all three throughout the day.)

❖ ❖ ❖ ❖ ❖

59   Love one another as I have loved you.
                                    —John 13:34

We couldn't be challenged more. We want to love. Deep down, we even want to give selfless love. Yet we love and find that the other won't receive our ways of loving. Or we find that our love isn't enough to "save" the other. Or we can't figure out what it is that the other needs to feel loved. And sometimes we feel inadequate or that our love is useless.

God calls us to love as Jesus loves.

Think of someone that you love, a person you have, at times, put ahead of yourself. Imagine God holding you in delight as you give that person love.

Think of someone who rejected or deflected your love. Or a relationship where some of your own less healthy needs got in the way. Or one in which you did not have the strength to give love when it was needed. Perhaps you loved, but were just unable to love enough. Whatever the reason, imagine God holding you, loving you and consoling you—as someone comforts a child who tries to walk and falls.

Offer gratitude today, for each gift of love the Spirit has enabled you to give, for all the fruits of your love that are known and unknown. Give thanks for your willingness to love even when your love did not seem to be the gift you wanted it to be in the other's life.

For Your Day: I want to love.

❖ ❖ ❖ ❖ ❖

60   Rejoice in God always; again I say, rejoice. God is near to you.

—Philippians 4:4,5

A button in my collection reminds me that "fun is the most important discipline of all." When Paul tells us to rejoice, I think he means: "Have a good time. God is in the world and in you. Let go of your grip and recognize that God wants you to take some leisure, some times to be peaceful and playful."

For some, play comes easily. More serious types need to "work up" to it. When we play, we are letting go of our control of the world, our ways of trying to make it better or avoid pain.

Play can be an attitude, a way of doing things, as well as a leisure time activity. We can try to take ourselves and our accomplishments with a lighter slant. We can do what we are able to do and let go of what is undone. We remind ourselves that the sun will rise and set without our thinking about it and that God will still be with us no matter what happens.

Think about how you can make today, even if you have many duties and responsibilities, a lighter day, a play day. Consider the spirit with which you will carry out your tasks or enjoy your leisure. Then make sure you do get some time today just for play.

For Your Day: I will play before my God.

❖ ❖ ❖ ❖ ❖

61   Child, get up!
                    —Luke 8:54

Jesus commands the daughter of Jairus to get up even though family and friends scoffed at him. They had declared her dead; Jesus said that she was sleeping. But the child does respond to Jesus' words and gets up to be embraced by her family.

Many a woman's inner child seemed to die early as she was forced to grow up too quickly. Parental illness, alcohol or drugs, may have done it. Her parents may have needed parenting themselves. Many a woman's inner child gets buried under responsibility taken on too early, or under emotional abandonment or heavy criticism.

If you are one of these women, listen to Jesus tell you that your inner child is sleeping, not dead. Hear him say to her, "Child, get up!" What does she do? What does Jesus do?

If your inner child was accepted and nurtured, consider with the compassion of Jesus those women you know who were not as fortunate. Ask that they be raised up again.

For Your Day: You hold out your hand to me.

God's Mercy Cleanses Me

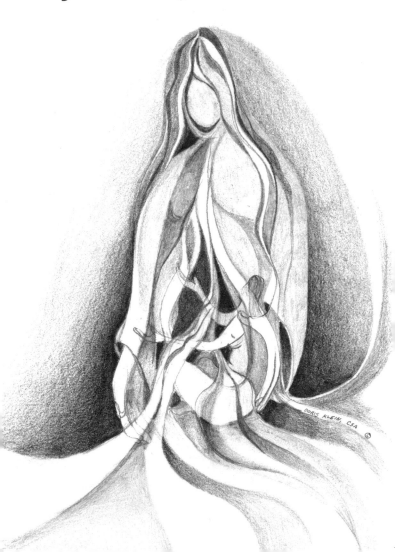

62 Even if your sins are scarlet,
    I will make you white as freshly fallen
      snow;
Even if they are crimson red,
    I will make you white as wool.
        —Isaiah 1:18

The difference between the greatest sinner and the greatest saint is only a millimeter compared to the chasm of the difference between either one and God. But God leaps over that abyss and takes both repentant sinner and gracious saint into the same welcoming arms. What is my response to this? Do I feel glad for both? Do I think of sinner and saint receiving the same embrace as unfair? Do I feel relieved?

Whether your sins are great or small, let God drop them down into a canyon which will swallow them up. Let God seal the sides together in one great tethering of nature and walk across that seam to sweep you up in a loving embrace. Let white light surround both you and God.

For Your Day: I am white as snow.

❖ ❖ ❖ ❖ ❖

63 A leper knelt before Jesus and said, "Lord, if you want to, you can make me clean." He stretched out his hand and touched him, saying, "Of course I want to. Be made clean!"
        —Matthew 8:2-3

With healthy guilt, we ask to be made clean from our sins. We also need cleansing of our unhealthy guilt and self-rejecting feelings. We seek cleansing of the poisonous guilt that we suffer for times when we have simply made a poor judgment; have been unable to resolve a conflict with someone; failed to live up to someone's expectation; had angry thoughts of revenge; forgot to stop at the hospital or write a card.

God waits to give us instant cleansing when we bring the sorrow and guilt of our sins. God washes us clean and lets the dirt become absorbed in an ocean of mercy, never to be found again. We can run and jump freely in God's loving radiance.

We don't need forgiveness for our mistakes, failures, faults, or temptations. What we need scrubbed away is our feelings of guilt about them. We need to let ourselves be cleansed of the false shame we have for being imperfect human beings.

Reread the passage as if you are the leper bringing to Jesus your healthy or unhealthy guilt for him to clean.

For Your Day: Hear God or Jesus saying to you: "Of course I want to. Be made clean."

❖ ❖ ❖ ❖ ❖

64   Jesus told the person freed from demons: "Go home and tell your friends what God has done for you, and the mercy God has shown you."

—Mark 5:19

Stories of devils, villians, the Loch Ness monster, and aggressors from outer space fascinate us. They mirror the shadows inside of us. We all have a few monsters or potential demons lurking within.

Demons may be parts of ourselves that refuse to submit to the God-self within and, instead, take over part or all of life. For instance, feeling jealous, angry, revengeful, empty, sexual, prejudiced, guilty, or lazy is normal. But if any of these spurns the counselling of one's whole self and takes over our behavior, it becomes a demon. When anything such as alcohol, gambling, self-hatred, or perfectionism controls us, it acts as a demon.

Consider any demons that have already been expelled in you. If you give credit to God, tell someone you trust about this. If you have never had occasion to expel a demon, reveal to someone today the mercy God has shown you. If you have a strong demon that needs to be expelled, rejoice in God who loves you and wants to cast it out with your consent and help.

For Your Day: Your mercy fills me always.

❖ ❖ ❖ ❖ ❖

65   My thoughts are not your thoughts,
      My ways are not your ways.
            —Isaiah 55:8

When we are hurt, our thoughts and actions often jump toward stinging words, petty judgments, and revenge. When we make decisions, our meager knowledge limits the horizons of our thoughts. When we plan, we can only take in the present and the future we can see.

Let us be thankful that our thoughts are not God's thoughts, our ways not God's ways. God loves us with total love even after we fail—unlike many of us who might retaliate, criticize, or judge another who failed us. God sees the ultimate meaning of our lives rather than just the partially worked crossword puzzle of the present.

Think of other ways that God's thoughts are not like your own.

For Your Day: I trust in *your* ways.

❖ ❖ ❖ ❖ ❖

66   Sing for joy, O heavens, exult, O earth;
    O mountains, break into singing;
For God comforts you,
    and has compassion on you who suffer.
          —Isaiah 49:13

Compassion means "to suffer with." We often suffer with our spouse, children, members of our family of origin, and our friends. We even suffer with our world neighbors when the violence, starvation, and oppression they endure confront us in the media. Some of us are drawn into others' sufferings through our compassion. So is God.

God comforts us. God comforts others. When we can, we offer our comfort to those in suffering. We can also give them God's promise of presence and deliverance—after we first receive it ourselves.

Do you need comforting at present? Can you give comfort to yourself? To whom can you turn today for some comfort? Resolve to ask for it. If you do not need comforting today, is there someone who needs yours? Resolve to give it if you can.

For Your Day: Comfort me and I will sing for joy.

❖ ❖ ❖ ❖ ❖

67   Do not be afraid; I have redeemed you.
I have called you by name; you are mine.
—Isaiah 43:1

Neither God nor Jesus advertises for followers by tacking notices on bulletin boards. God calls each of us by name to hear the Good News of love and redemption.

Prompted from within yourself or from a source outside, you have been drawn to search for God, to thirst for Ultimate Meaning, to desire to lay down your life in surrender to One who calls and embraces you with unconditional love. You are not a random choice. You have been called by name.

Repeat the verse from Isaiah aloud to yourself many times. Place your own name in the first line after the word *afraid* and in the second after *name*. If possible, ask someone else to read it to you a few times this way.

For Your Day: You have called me by name. I am yours.

❖ ❖ ❖ ❖ ❖

68   Even if you have been dead through sin, God is rich in mercy and with great love for you makes you alive together with Christ. By grace, you are saved through faith. This is the gift of God, not your own doing.

—Ephesians 2:5, 8

Some of us have been dead because of sin; others severely or lightly injured by sin. The differences do not matter. We have all failed through actions or omissions, compulsions or addictions, rage or apathy to respond to "the great love with which God loves." No need, however, to even mention your failings. You are raised up by God's love and grace.

Imagine yourself standing in a gorgeous white dress before Jesus, raised up beside him. Nothing stands between you and God. Dare to claim your own resurrection and freedom flowing from God's gift. Walk and talk with Jesus about the goodness of your life.

For Your Day: I am rich in mercy.

❖ ❖ ❖ ❖ ❖

69   Woman, you are free of your illness.

—Luke 13:12

Jesus frees the bent-over woman who, for eighteen years, has been unable to stand up straight. Jesus wants to free women today who, after almost two thousand years of Christianity, are still bent over and unable to offer the fullness of their gifts to society and the church.

Did it take courage for the woman to stand up at Jesus' words? Was she afraid of the new role she would now play in her family and society? Of the responsibility she would be taking on? Would she lose some of the security and protection she had in her illness? Perhaps some sympathy? Would she, maybe, stand alone?

Do you feel bent down in any way by patriarchal society? If you stood up, how would your life change? What negatives would you meet face to face? If you do not feel bent over, listen to some women who do. Are you willing to care about them, to do something to help them straighten up?

Read the whole passage (Luke 13:10-17) and imagine the feelings of the woman. Note the way others respond to Jesus when he heals her.

For Your Day: Hear Jesus say to you: "Woman, you are free."

❖ ❖ ❖ ❖ ❖

70   I will place my Spirit in you and you will live.
I will put you down on you own soil and you will know that
I, your God, have done as I have promised.
—Ezekiel 37:14

Sometimes I ask people if they think we will be reincarnated. The most usual response is, "Whew,

I hope not!" It seems that even though people do not regret the life they are in, they have experienced enough suffering and difficulty not to want another go-around.

Recall a time when you thought you were dying—spiritually, psychologically, or physically. Did it seem as if life would always carry the pain, the heaviness, the shame, the confusion you were feeling? What helped you survive? What made the difference?

Read again God's promise to you though the prophet Ezekiel. Know that God wants you to live. God is always ready to place the Spirit within you so that you can rise again. God will "place you on your own soil," on the solid ground within you where you meet your deepest self and the One who loves you there.

For Your Day: Thank you for the power of your Spirit in me.

❖ ❖ ❖ ❖ ❖

71   Take my yoke upon yourself and learn from me. I am gentle and humble of heart and you will find rest. My yoke is easy and my burden light.

—Matthew 11:29-30

In this passage, Jesus releases us from the *burden* of the law and invites us to accept his yoke instead. His yoke binds us to listen to the voice of God and obey it. Since when is this yoke of listening easy?

Or this burden of obedience light?

This yoke of obedience led Jesus to criticize the hypocrisy of his religious leaders, cure a suffering person instead of keeping the sabbath law, walk and eat with people whom society despised, and speak with authority about religious matters even though he was not a rabbi. The yoke burdened him with a cruel and violent death.

Yet, the yoke of listening to God also led Jesus to liberation. Others saw his freedom and longed for it. They felt the strength and courage flowing from his freedom and witnessed even his release from death. In this freedom, the yoke is easy and the burden light.

Think of the freedom to which Jesus calls you as you feel the weight of your own yokes—your unrealistic expectations of yourself or expectations that you believe others have of you. Look for ways to remove these burdens and step forward in freedom as Jesus did.

For Your Day: I will take up your yoke.

❖ ❖ ❖ ❖ ❖

72 In God you live, and move, and exist.
—Acts 17:28

God is closer to us than we are to ourselves. We live and move in God. We shrink from taking in this truth, believing in it and trying to live it because intimacy is so frightening. We approach intimacy with other persons slowly, testing the water, seeing if the other can be trusted with our wounds and weaknesses. We even have difficulty entrusting ourselves to God.

Think about any way in which your life would be different if you accepted God's intimacy, if you lived in awareness of God's all encompassing presence. Think about how it might affect your relationships with others.

For Your Day: I live and move in you.

❖ ❖ ❖ ❖ ❖

73   Do you know that you are a temple of God and a dwelling place of the Spirit? You are God's temple and God's temple is holy.
                              —1 Corinthians 3:16-17

Temples are set aside as special places. God's presence makes them holy places. Yet, temples are not perfect. They have structural weaknesses and their surfaces wear down. Heat, cold, and wind scar and discolor their walls.

Imagine your body and spirit as God's temple, filled with God's light and radiance, a welcoming place for the Spirit. Recognize that your body as it is, not as the advertising industry would have it, is a house of God. Consider your goodness, not measured against some abstract scale of perfection, but as you are. Express your love to God within you, within your own body and person.

For Your Day: To the Holy Spirit: I worship you within me.

❖ ❖ ❖ ❖ ❖

74   What do you want me to do for you?
                              —Mark 10:51

Hear this *carte blanche* invitation to state your deepest desire, your direst need. Can you imagine that anyone should sincerely ask this question and hear Jesus reply, "Sorry, that's too much for me to do"? In earlier years, though, some of us heard this reply verbally or nonverbally when we expressed our needs. Our overly stressed or overly tired parents let us know that what we wanted was too much trouble. So now we find it difficult, sometimes impossible, to ask for help, to believe that we won't be too much bother. If so, asking for God's help, answering Jesus' question above, becomes formidable. Some may be tempted to ask only for a small favor, a big one being "too much trouble" or "too presumptuous."

Relax for a few minutes and then let Jesus ask you the question above. You have nothing to fear from Jesus. How do you respond?

For Your Day: "Jesus, I want you to . . . ."

❖ ❖ ❖ ❖ ❖

75   Heaven celebrates with more joy over one
        sinner who is sorry than over ninety-nine
        righteous persons who do not need to repent.
                              —Luke 15:7

When we have hurt someone we love, the pain inside can become unbearable. When we have hurt ourselves by making a poor decision, missing an opportunity, or misusing our bodies we feel a heaviness inside. Yet to God, nothing is irreparable. We need to ask forgiveness of another, grieve our mistakes, forgive ourselves, and be open to the compassion of God instead of the condemnation we may be tempted to lay on ourselves.

All of heaven and earth celebrate when you receive the mercy of God. Are you feeling any sadness right now because you need forgiveness? Do you need God's compassion, the forgiveness of another, or your own forgiveness? Remember that whatever you have done is negligible compared to the person of great value that you are. Trust in your value as God does.

For Your Day: I will live in forgiveness.

❖ ❖ ❖ ❖ ❖

76   I will take the heart of stone out of your body and give you a heart of flesh. I will put my spirit within you. I will be your God.
—Ezekiel 35:26-28

Ezekiel's symbol of a heart of stone has become almost a cliché. In every generation, hardness of heart is experienced personally and collectively.

This passage offers a relief, a cure! It is God who will soften my resisting heart. God will give me the "care-full" heart I need to love myself, forgive myself, to nurture my child within when it needs support or play. God will make it possible for me to cherish my body, devotedly giving it good food and sufficient rest.

What is God's Spirit whispering to you right now about caring for yourself, about getting what you need?

Take a rock or stone and mark a word or symbol on it to suggest what needs to be changed in you. Or draw a heart on paper and place the words or a symbol in it. Offer this in prayer, counting on God to change you.

For Your Day: Put your Spirit within me.

❖ ❖ ❖ ❖ ❖

77   May the God of peace sanctify you; and may your spirit, soul and body be kept safe and blameless for the coming of our Lord Jesus Christ. God calls you and God is faithful.
                                    —2 Thessalonians 5:23-24

When words such as *sanctify entirely* and *blameless* refer to us, we squirm. Which of us can even come near being entirely holy and blameless? Yet the Bible asks us to believe that we can.

The passage above tells us that it is God who sanctifies and who keeps us blameless. If God carries no blame for our failures, why do we? Can anyone point a finger? If God makes us holy, then how can we protest that we are not? God sees us holy and blameless; can we see ourselves this way?

Can we believe it and rejoice in it?

Remember the worst thing you have done in your life and say aloud to God that you believe it is wiped away—and all your lesser crimes with it. Sit in the awareness of your radiant beauty in God's loving light. Then reread the last sentence of the scripture quotation.

For Your Day: You are faithful to me.

❖ ❖ ❖ ❖ ❖

78   God is waiting to be gracious to you;
          to rise up to show mercy to you.
                        —Isaiah 30:18

The prophet Isaiah pictures God as waiting for us. Waiting for us to do what? Finish cleaning the house? Complete the portfolio? Conclude the fund raiser for the homeless? Retire from a job to have time to pray? Be perfect in our own minds before we turn to God?

"God is waiting to be gracious to you," the prophet says. All God needs—even in the midst of our busyness—is for us to acknowledge that we need mercy and want to receive it. God is waiting for us to ask. God is ready and waiting to give us mercy.

Consider the ways that you need God's mercy. Are you willing to receive it? To let go of self-recrimination or guilt? To forgive yourself? God waits to be gracious (to give the gift) to you. For today, let go of the past and let God be loving to you.

For Your Day: You are gracious and merciful to me.

❖ ❖ ❖ ❖ ❖

79 Jesus prayed: Make her one with us as you
    are in me and I am in you.
                            —John 17:22

Jesus prays that we may be one with each other and one with him and God. Jesus does not say, "When they become perfect, when they no longer struggle with sin, selfishness and addictions, make them one with us." Nor does Jesus pray that we all be one in the next world. He is speaking of union with us now, just as we are.

The union to which Jesus calls us can happen now because God's love washes away our sin and imperfection and invites us to do the same for one another. Lest we see the ideal as too great, Jesus asks the Spirit of God to give us the power to love in this way. Let us claim that power.

Recognize Jesus' desire for oneness with you just as you are. Picture other people you know, those whom you love, those whom you find unattractive. Recognize Jesus' desire for oneness with each of them. Ask for the power to love others just as they are. Ask for the power to love yourself just as you are.

For Your Day: May we all be one.

80   A woman who had been suffering from hemorrhages for twelve years had spent all she had on physicians. No one could cure her. She came up behind Jesus and touched the fringe of his cloak. Immediately her hemorrhage stopped.

Jesus said to her, "Daughter, your faith has made you well. Go in peace."

—Luke 8:43-44, 48

How often we have listened to stories of women going to doctor after doctor and getting no help! Especially if the person has a "female illness," she finds that little research has been done on the matter or that she is not believed. Then she is patted on the head with an indication that all will be well if she just calms down. Perhaps the way doctors treated the woman with a hemorrhage left her afraid to approach Jesus. She did not have the courage to go forward and ask for a cure. But Jesus always took women seriously, here and in other places recorded in the gospels. Jesus meets each of us, our degree of faith and our illnesses, with respect.

If you have ever felt discounted by another person about an illness, an addiction, a compulsion, or a fear, ask Jesus to come and sit beside you. Tell him the story. If you are in need of healing, reach over and touch his cloak, telling him you believe that he can heal you both your illness and the hurt feelings you have suffered at the hands of others because of it. If you can, read the whole story of this woman's healing in Luke 8:43-48.

For Your Day: If I but touch the fringe of your cloak, I will be healed.

❖ ❖ ❖ ❖ ❖

81   God has saved my soul from going down into the pit, and I shall see the light.
—Job 33:28

Who has not heard the saying, "Life is the pits"? Most of us, like Job, feel like that sometimes. We are uncomfortable with the mystery that some fall into pits more often than others. But an even greater mystery is that some who have climbed out of one burning and charring pit after another can still glow with love, compassion, and gentleness. The descent of others, even to lesser depths, leaves them sometimes bitter, often hostile, and always complaining.

Perhaps some keep a higher part of themselves from descending into the depths. Others may fall completely into sadness and terror. Yet, through faith, they never lose the light of God's ever-present love. God never promised that we wouldn't suffer. Jesus certainly got the worst. God promised, however, to walk with us and to remind us repeatedly that resurrections follow deaths. That is light, indeed.

Consider how you have emerged from your pits. Let God's light shine on you, embrace you, and heal you. If you linger down in the depths right now, let Job remind you that light is present to you, even if you cannot yet see it.

For Your Day: You always redeem me.

God Strengthens Me

82   Come to the throne of grace with boldness, so that you will have mercy and help in time of need.

—Hebrews 4:16

Society frowns on bold women. It assigns derogatory adjectives: brazen, aggressive, shrill. The word *bold* coupled with *woman* is intended to degrade, though it is often taken as a compliment when it describes a *man*. God does not have society's hang-ups. The scriptures tell us to reach deep inside of ourselves to name our deepest needs and to bring them *boldly* to God. God loves a woman's fearless, daring spirit and rewards it.

If you know the stories of Esther, Mary Magdalene, Hildegard of Bingen, Dorothy Day, and other *bold* women, invite their spirits to be with you today.

Take a few minutes to breathe deeply. Imagine you are going down inside yourself on an elevator. As you descend, count the floors down 10, 9, 8 . . . to one. Walk out of the elevator and face an ornate door. Walk through it to discover before you your deepest need. Take it back up with you, counting in reverse as you go up. When you open the elevator, see before you the throne or the light of God. Bring your need boldly before God expecting the mercy promised you.

For Your Day: I come boldly before you.

❖ ❖ ❖ ❖ ❖

83
I will go before you,
   leveling the mountains.
I will shatter the doors of bronze
   and snap the bars of iron.
I will give you the treasures stored in
    darkness
   and riches hidden in secret places.
     —Isaiah 45:2-3

To reach the lands of riches and treasures, we may have to cross formidable barriers: an addiction or compulsion, a physical illness, an emotional weakness, fear, an inner resistance to change, overwork, or scattered energies.

Our barriers become God's challenges. The burden of breaking through to treasures on the shadowed side of ourselves does not rest on us. God promises to go before us and cut the path.

Imagine God tearing down the bronze doors of your barrier, cutting through the iron parts of it. Visualize the treasures and riches on the other side.

For Your Day: You go before me.

❖ ❖ ❖ ❖ ❖

84
I have put my words in your mouth,
And covered you in the shadow of my hand.
     —Isaiah 51:16

As incredible as it seems, God depends on each of us to speak what needs to be said. What words does God put into our mouths? Words of comfort, encouragement, love. Words of defense for the helpless, the slandered, the judged. Words of confrontation for those whose sharp tongues spew sarcasm, lies, and condemnation. Words of anger to those who gain their own wealth or power at the expense of others. Words of reconciliation for those who have hurt and been hurt.

Often we know the words of God that fill our mouths, but we fear the consequences of speaking them. What keeps you from speaking them at times? Remember the promise of God's protection. You live in the shadow of God's hand.

Remember a time when you have spoken God's words.

For Your Day: I will speak your words.

❖ ❖ ❖ ❖ ❖

85 Do not let your heart be troubled. Trust in God and trust in me.
—John 14:1

Our hearts get heaped up with trouble. We worry about what's happening to our children, symptoms of illness in a spouse or parent, having enough money to pay off the credit cards, hurting someone's feelings at a meeting, what to have for dinner for friends, whether a supervisor approves of our work, or what we can do about hunger in Africa. No end to troubles.

What kinds of things do you tend to worry about most? Name them and then listen to the words of Jesus to you.

Each time worry tempts you today, cup your hands and imagine the trouble cradled in your palms. Open your hands and let the trouble fall through.

For Your Day: I trust in you.

❖ ❖ ❖ ❖ ❖

86   God gives power to the weak,
         And strength to the powerless.
                        —Isaiah 40:29

Sometimes we turn every piece around and check every angle, trying to get the puzzles of our relationships to fit together. But the pieces don't always seem to come together into a satisfying picture.

Sometimes we drive down a different road to prevent a wreck—in our lives or in the lives of those we love—only to watch helplessly as the crash occurs anyway.

Sometimes our inner resources are not sufficient for making wise decisions, taking the actions that might resolve a dilemma.

We are tempted then to tighten our grip of control even more. In doing so, we can block the energy of God-Within-Us. When we acknowledge our inabilities, our fragility, we can call upon and receive power beyond our own. When we face our powerlessness, strength will be given us.

Remember a time in the past when you received strength or power beyond your own. How did you feel when you recognized this? Consider that God is faithful to you and can give you that same power and strength, today and tomorrow.

For Your Day: Strengthen me with your power.

❖ ❖ ❖ ❖ ❖

87 You who wait for God
shall renew your strength,
you will take off with eagles' wings.
you will walk and not get tired,
you will run and not faint.
—Isaiah 40:31

I know people who will drive miles out of their way to avoid a long traffic light. Most of us just don't like to wait. Of course we do end up tapping our fingers fairly often. We wait with frustrated sighs in grocery lines and traffic jams. We wait in anxious fear when a loved one does not arrive on time. We wait with tightening jaws for a doctor's report. We would rather do anything than just wait.

Yet, the Bible calls us to wait for our God who will renew our strength. The reward is worth it. Our search for God will soar with the power of eagles' wings. We will not grow weary of seeking the meaning of our lives. We will walk the long distance of learning to love ourselves and others—and not grow faint.

Read carefully what is promised to you if you wait for God.

For Your Day: I wait for you to renew my strength.

❖ ❖ ❖ ❖ ❖

88   I know the plans I have in mind for you, plans for your good, not for harm, offering a future full of hope for you.

—Jeremiah 29:11

God works within us. Today. This minute. For our good. Through the prophet, we are assured that God wants only what is good for us. The words continue to reinforce that most strengthening of gifts—hope.

Think about how God works for your good, today and every day of your life: that inner voice that urges you to speak the kind word even while the impatient one is sneaking onto your tongue; an understanding nod from a friend; the courage to speak up when silence would be easier; a flower in the grass or cactus on the sand demanding that you stop and admire them; someone's hug. How did God work for your good in the past twenty-four hours? Rest in the "love-liness" of God's goodness to you.

For Your Day: As you become aware of the eyes, the voice, and the embrace of God working for your good today, pray frequently: Strengthen me in hope.

❖ ❖ ❖ ❖ ❖

89

God heals broken hearts
and binds up wounds.

—Psalm 147:3

Over and over again our hearts cry out for healing.
The death of someone we love severs the heart. The
demise of a marriage, a friendship, or a dream
smashes it. Sharp words, dull indifference, and
aloof ingratitude wound it.

Picture God as glowing light. Imagine the light
filling and healing your heart of all its present and
past ruptures. Stay immersed in that light as it
warms you and binds up your wounds.

If you are suffering physical illness, let this light
surround and penetrate the sick part of your body.
Image it as warming those parts and healing them.

For Your Day: You heal my broken heart and bind
up all my wounds.

❖ ❖ ❖ ❖ ❖

90

I can do all things in God who strengthens
me.

—Philippians 4:13

Can we say these words of ourselves? Or do we
retreat into a cave of fear when we see trouble
rumbling down our rocky path? When we are
called on to care for a sick child or parent, when we
must struggle through our own temporary or
chronic illness, when we must confront someone
we love, when we lose a job, when we must parent

alone, God calls us to believe that the strengthening Spirit lives within us.

Repeat the words of Paul aloud to see if you mean them.

What is the hardest task facing you, the most difficult circumstance in your life at present? See or feel God's strength within you giving you the power to endure, or respond, or initiate. If you cannot feel it, keep repeating the passage. Remember that God does the strengthening, not you.

For Your Day: I can do all things in you who strengthen me.

❖ ❖ ❖ ❖ ❖

91 In hope you were saved. If you see what you hope for, you do not need hope. For who hopes for what is seen? You hope for what you do not see and wait for it with patience.
—Romans 8:24

Loss of hope is the worst loss possible. As hope deteriorates, so does our ability to envision possibilities and our energy to change the situation. Total loss of hope plunges us into a chasm of despair and we no longer want to live. Sometimes the flame of hope gets buried so deeply that we cannot even remember that we have it. We no longer cry for help because we do not believe anything or anyone can help us.

God, who desires our fullness of life, uncovers the buried flame and fans it into fire through the

Word. Sometimes we receive it in the faithful love of others, sometimes through God's words. No one's black night lasts forever.

Remember a time when hope seemed only an ember. Also remember a time when all of nature seemed to burst into song for you. Not being able to bask in the light does not mean that it isn't glowing. Thank God for bringing you out of seemingly hopeless situations of the past or for constantly giving you so much hope so that you haven't had to experience the darkness that goes with its loss. Reread the passage above several times.

For Your Day: I hope in you.

❖ ❖ ❖ ❖ ❖

92   I am your God who comforts you;
why then are you afraid of some mere
human being who must die,
someone who fades like grass?
—Isaiah 51:12

The logic is s-o-o-o-o logical. Indeed, why should we be afraid of others who are just human beings like us? But do you know of any woman without fear? An alarmingly high percentage of girls and women face sexual abuse, incest, rape, sexual harassment, and physical battering. More live with low self-esteem and other psychological damage from contempt, betrayal, job discrimination, enforced financial insecurity, or poverty. All women—and men—risk hurt, rejection, and hostile persecution by some other.

We respond: "We are afraid, God, because we suffer." And like Jesus, we want to say, "Let this chalice pass."

God does not reply by taking away the results of the evil we experience or the possibilities of future anguish. Instead, God strengthens us by walking with us in the suffering. "I am your God who comforts you."

Spend a few minutes letting the following words become a part of you: In whatever happens to me today, I walk in the comfort of your presence. I know your love and strength will sustain me.

For Your Day: Your love and strength sustain me.

❖ ❖ ❖ ❖ ❖

93   My grace is enough for you: my power will work perfectly in your weakness.

—2 Corinthians 12:9

Acknowledging a particular weakness sets our feet on a road to wholeness and holiness. (Both words come from the same Anglo-Saxon root, *hol*, which means health.) Denying a weakness creates tension and makes us so afraid of others' opinions that we become too rigid to move. Wallowing in our weakness by laying guilt on ourselves or judging ourselves as inadequate leaves us in a rut. By accepting our frailty, we sprint straight down the road to the gates of the city of God where our weakness can be transformed.

When we can let go of trying to overcome weakness with our own strength or will power, the power of God can take over. We know that God has always held on to us even when we thought we could hold on no more. We find we have all we need—to overcome or accept our problems, fears, and grief.

Can you think of an example of what God has already done in your own life? Do you have a weakness that needs to be turned over to God's power now?

For Your Day: Your grace is enough for me.

❖ ❖ ❖ ❖ ❖

94 The Spirit will help you when you do not know how to pray as you ought. The Spirit will intercede with prayers too deep for words. God searches hearts and knows the mind of the Spirit who intercedes for everyone according to the will of God.

—Romans 8:26-27

Ordinarily prayerful women and men who have just had surgery often complain, "I just can't pray." Anyone who has experienced serious illness, or even a few days of flu, knows how hard, almost impossible, it is to concentrate during that time. We also find prayer difficult when tension, depression, fear, or worry weakens us.

Let yourself be consoled in knowing that the Spirit of God is praying in you even when you cannot bring the desired thoughts or words to mind. The prayer within you will be in accord with God's will. You know that God's will is your good and the good of all for whom you would like to pray.

Breathe in and out slowly several times. Become conscious of the Spirit of God as one with your breath. Follow it and let go of thinking any thoughts. Let the Spirit intercede for you. No matter how you feel today, ask the Spirit of God to pray in you. Let go of your own prayer agenda.

For Your Day: Spirit of God, pray in me.

❖ ❖ ❖ ❖ ❖

95   Peace I leave with you; my own peace I give to you. I do not give you the kind of peace that the world gives.
                                                    —John 14:27

The world gives peace and takes it away. The world promises that peace can be secured through cash, property, a position of power, health, or pleasure. Yet most of us can name people who are immensely rich with those "treasures" who still lack inward peace. This fact, however, seldom stops us from feeling that one of them would bring peace in our lives. Sometimes we focus our lives on going after them. We need to be reminded that Jesus also said, "Where your treasure is, there your heart will also be" (Luke 12:34).

Tell Jesus what gives you real peace. Is it trusting that God will give you, or others, what you need to get through difficulty? Feeling at one with God? Feeling at one with those with whom you live and work? Knowing you are so deeply loved that eventually God will bring about all things for your good?

Imagine Jesus standing before you, looking into your eyes and telling you personally the gospel words above. Ask him what he means by them.

For Your Day: Hear Jesus saying to you throughout the day, "*My* peace I give to you."

❖ ❖ ❖ ❖ ❖

96   Do not worry about anything, but let your requests be made known to God with prayers of petition and thanksgiving.
—Philippians 4:4-6

My friend Shirley was feeling blue: "I just wish I could be happy-go-lucky like other people."

"Whom do you have in mind?" I asked.

"Well . . . well . . . ." She started to laugh.

"Well?"

"I can't think of anyone."

Some happy-go-lucky people live on sitcoms. But for those of us who are living off camera, life dishes out lots of troublesome situations. Can you think of any normal person who doesn't feel sad or worried at times? Some worry normally and some worry too much.

Yet Paul's encouragement is for both groups: "Do not worry." He gives us an alternative—pray. Talk to God about your needs. "Let go! Let God!" is a popular way of putting it. In a way, this all seems too simple. But it is the word of God which is challenging us. Each step toward trusting without worrying is a move toward the freedom of the daughters and sons of God.

Let go of any worries, no matter how serious or how small, that are on your mind for today. Give them a symbol such as a cloud or a rock. Pick up your worry symbol and, if it is light, let it float to God. Do not take it back today. If it is heavy, hand it to God or put it in a place for God to come and get it. Do not go back for it today.

For Your Day: I am letting go of my worries.

❖ ❖ ❖ ❖ ❖

97   In your faithful love you lead me whom
        you have saved;
     by your strength you guide me to
        your dwelling place.
                     —Exodus 15:13

Where is God's "dwelling place" for you? A place in the center of yourself? In time spent with someone you love? A spot in nature where you feel the presence of God? Heaven? All of the above?

This passage offers wonderful words to lift the pressure from those of us who often try too hard to earn our salvation or believe ourselves unworthy of it. We hold in our hearts the words, *your steadfast love, you guide me, your strength*. We can let go of our *self*-consciousness and let *God* lead, redeem, guide, and strengthen. We can let God take us home to our "dwelling place."

Remember a time when you felt stuck in your journey home—to yourself, to God. Perhaps you couldn't get past a bad habit, get out of an unhealthy relationship, couldn't forgive. Were you ever *led* out of the cave when you could struggle no more? Turn over to God today whatever keeps you from coming home. Expect God to lead you.

For Your Day: I will trust in *your* (choose one) love, guidance, strength.

❖ ❖ ❖ ❖ ❖

98 I want to see again.
—Mark 10:51

Some might say, "I want to *be* again." Because of our early upbringing, most of us have parts of ourselves that were squashed down, poked out, blinded. For some of us, anger was not to be shown or even experienced. Not if we were to be *nice* little girls. For others, sadness was eclipsed with, "Now, smile!" Or we were not to show the fear we felt in going to the first grade, to the dentist, to the hospital. "I want you to be a brave little girl," meant, "Don't show any feelings that I will have to deal with."

What part of yourself do you still hold down with some leftover inner tapes from childhood?

What part of you needs to see daylight again? What part of you needs to be integrated so that you may be healed, may be made whole again?

Speak to Jesus of your need for healing.

For Your Day: Let me _____ again.

❖ ❖ ❖ ❖ ❖

99   No one can come to me unless she is drawn by God who sent me; and I will raise her up on the last day.

—John 6:44

When have you felt drawn by God? How? When you wanted to love and be loved? When you felt gratitude or adoration? When you realized a power within you greater than your own? When you began your search for spiritual truth? When you experienced awe in nature? You would not be holding this book if you had not been drawn to God in faith or hope.

As much as you want to love God and to feel yourself loved in return, so infinitely more does God desire it for you. God wants you to *experience* the love so that you live life abundantly. As one who has been drawn by God, you can be confident that God will continue to draw you.

Knowing you are loved so totally, think about the promise given you in the passage above. Does this promise affect your life and the way you think about it? If so, in what way?

For Your Day: Thank you for drawing me to you.

❖ ❖ ❖ ❖ ❖

100 Live in my love.
—John 15:9

We are not only called to believe in the love God gives us, but to dwell in it as well. We are to go about our work, talk with others, and choose our activities immersed in that love. We are called to swim in it as dolphin pirouette in the water. How would your day be different if you lived in this way?

Before you begin your next activity, stop to breathe deeply. With each breath take in love, the love of God that you have come to know in Jesus. As you exhale, dispel feelings of aloneness. Know that you are moving, swimming, in the ocean of God's love.

For Your Day: You live in me and I in you.

❖ ❖ ❖ ❖ ❖

101 You received without paying; give without receiving payment.
—Matthew 10:8

When we receive an honest compliment, a word of praise, or a loving nod of appreciation, we light up inside. We gain renewed energy and bloom with enthusiasm. Although God's constant love is available and we do receive some affirmation from others, can we ever get enough? We *can* increase what we receive and what we give. In God's love, we can give light, energy, and enthusiasm (*en-thu* means *with God*) to others. It will return to us.

Think of the persons with whom you live and those you will be meeting today. What compliment, word of praise, or appreciation can you give to them? Begin with yourself. Compliment or praise yourself aloud for three different things. Make this a day of giving freely what you have received.

For Your Day: I am wonderful. I will let others know that they are wonderful, too.